FINDING HOPE

IN THE MIDST OF TRAGEDY

Shelley Hitz

Finding Hope in the Midst of Tragedy

Copyright © 2009, 2012 by Shelley Hitz

All rights reserved. No part of this publication may be reproduced, stored in a retrieval system, or transmitted by any means – electronic, mechanical, photographic (photocopying), recording, or otherwise – without prior permission in writing from the author, unless it is for the furtherance of the Gospel of salvation and given away free of charge.

Body and Soul Publishing
ISBN-13: 978-0615681290
ISBN-10: 0615681298

All scripture quotations, unless otherwise indicated, are taken from the Holy Bible, New International Version® 1973, 1978, 1984 by International Bible Society. Used by permission of Zondervan Publishing House. All rights reserved.

Learn more information at:
www.BodyandSoulPublishing.com

Dedication

This book is dedicated to my dad, Chuck Sandstrom, and my step-mom, Auburn. Together, we have watched miracles take place over the last several years as God has touched our lives with His healing power: physically, emotionally and spiritually. With their permission, I now share our story with you.

Table of Contents

Introduction 1

Part One - Facing the Unknown 5

Part Two - A Glimmer of Hope 11

Part Three - A Foundation of Hope 35

Part Four - Day by Day 53

Part Five - Hope Breaks Through 87

Part Six - A New Beginning 127

Part Seven - The Hope Continues 159

About the Author: Shelley Hitz 167

Index of Entries 170

References 174

Introduction

I recently heard the word hope described as this acronym: Hold On, Pain Ends. And I have found that to be so true in my own life. One of my heroes of the faith and Nazi prison camp survivor, Corrie ten Boom, describes it this way, "When a train goes through a tunnel and it gets dark, you don't throw away the ticket and jump off. You sit still and trust the engineer."

This book is my own personal journey to finding hope after a tragedy hit our family. However, I did not want this book to be my story alone. Instead, I wanted it to be a resource for you to find hope in the midst of your own difficulties. That is why I have added the sections that you will see through the book called, "From My Life to Yours," where I add journaling prompts and suggested prayers for you to apply what you are learning to your life. I pray that God leads you to find His hope no matter what you are walking through.

My Story

I had no clue how drastically my life would change this year. I thought some of my worst days were over. I thought that I had dealt with enough trials for one lifetime. However, on July 1st 2009, that all changed when my dad, Chuck Sandstrom, was assaulted. Once again, a violent act was committed against our family and this time it hit even closer to home, my dad. Dad was assaulted so severely that it left him in a coma for almost six weeks and resulted in a severe Traumatic Brain Injury (TBI).

At first I was in shock and was numb. But, eventually, many emotions began to surface. Anger, grief, pain, unforgiveness. I heard myself saying, "Lord, it's not fair. Why our family, AGAIN? I don't know if I can handle this." I realized it was time for me to walk through the path of forgiveness once again and choose to trust God with the pain, the hurt and the unknowns of this tragedy. And He led me down a path to find hope...hope in the midst of tragedy.

I won't lie to you. It hasn't been an easy road. And it's not over. Dad is now out of the coma and progressing every day. He is walking, talking and eating again. He is now home. But, there is a long road ahead. Dad still needs a lot of speech therapy and cognitive therapy. He may end up losing his job. And they still haven't found his perpetrator. Yes, there is still a long road ahead of us. But, looking back, I can see God's Presence with us every step of the way. Every tear, every emotion, every joy, every disappointment. He has been here.

I've found out once again that what Jesus teaches is applicable to real-life. In the midst of pain, tragedy and some of the most difficult days of my life, Jesus brought me hope.
And He wants to do the same for you, if you'll seek Him and apply His teachings to your life.

What I share in this book in my "journal" that I posted on my blog through the difficult days after my dad's assault, coma and resulting traumatic brain injury. I opened my heart for all to see my journey...my journey to finding hope in the midst of tragedy. I pray God uses this book to encourage and inspire you.

My Dad and I on Father's Day

Dad and I During His Recovery

(The last time I saw him before his assault)

(Taken just shortly after he came out of the coma)

Part One

Facing the Unknown

July 1, 2009: About My Dad's Assault

On July 1st, 2009 my dad was assaulted and suffered a severe traumatic brain injury (TBI) that left him in a coma for weeks. We didn't know if he would survive that first day and then the doctors told us that he might never wake up. However, we have seen God work miracles in the midst of this tragedy.

The Media...

The first article printed in the media about Dad was in the Barberton Herald. Several other stories were published later in the Akron Beacon Journal, Channel 5 News and the Findlay Courier. However, as usually happens with news stories, all the details were not 100% accurate.

Here are a couple items to clear up...

There was a vehicle parked at my dad's rental property that was not registered to his tenants. It had been there for weeks and he decided to call the police and have it towed.

My dad's assailant, Michael, was not a tenant but a relative of a tenant. And witnesses say my dad was not in an argument. According to neighbors, Dad was attempting to reason with a highly volatile person about the towing of this unregistered vehicle that had been on the premises for weeks. Basically, he was a landlord taking care of business on his property.

Michael has a long list of previous arrests, many of them containing violence. He is known to have a bad temper. The police came twice prior to dad's assault. The first time, Michael left and the police left. The second time, they arrived after Michael left the scene. The third time was after dad's assault. Apparently, Michael hit dad several times on the front landing of his apartment building. It was loud enough for the neighbors to hear. There was a brick wall close by and we assume he hit his head on that brick wall at some point in the assault.

Everyone in the neighborhood have only good things to say about my dad and love my dad. They are all very sorry for what happened.

Dad's medical status...

Dad's initial medical status was that he was unconscious with a very severe brain injury. According to Akron General brain surgeons, prognosis can be 100% recovery with time.

The following link is to a helpful story on brain injury and recovery: http://www.parade.com/health/2009/07/12-lee-woodruff-can-brains-be-saved.html

The criminal case

I have stayed in close communication with the detectives on his case and they have activated the fugitive task force, which means there are US marshals looking for Michael as well. There is a warrant for his arrest and witnesses to the crime. Crime stoppers also has a reward for information leading to his arrest.

Thank you for your prayers and support! My step-mom, Auburn, has a blog she will be updating. You can see her updates at: http://www.chuckscircleoflove.com.

From My Life to Yours

Has your family been through something tragic that changed your life? Your experience might be completely different from ours, but any tragedy can be life altering. I encourage you to reflect on an incident from your own life that you are still struggling to understand as you read through our story. You can ponder the answers, or even start a journal like I did, and hopefully God can use what He taught me during those dark days to help you as well.

~ The first thing I encourage you to reflect on is the facts. What do you know to be true? Take some time and write them down, and then pray for God to help you understand what He is teaching you through these events.

July 23, 2009: Visiting Pity City

I am struggling today. One of my patients is a survivor of breast cancer and was sharing her story with me. She mentioned something helpful to me today. She said "I can visit 'pity city'…I just can't live there." I have to admit I felt like moving into "pity city" today! But, her words came at just the right time to remind me that it's okay to feel my feelings, but just not to let them control me. I have so much to learn…

July 23, 2009: Breakthrough to Hope

I felt like I had a breakthrough this morning. As I was journaling and praying, I felt God say to me that I need to focus on this being a transformational time for dad, emotionally and spiritually, and not to focus on what his physical and cognitive deficits will be as he recovers - that at the end of life, only one thing really matters…and that is our soul.

I have had peace and a sense from God from the beginning that Dad is okay. That his soul and spirit are okay and that Jesus is with him… that no matter what happens to him physically, Jesus is with him and is taking care of him. He is in good hands.

As I was praying this morning, God brought a scripture to my mind that I will now continue to hold on to for the duration of Dad's recovery. It is 2 Corinthians 4:16-18,

> *"Therefore we do not lose heart. Though outwardly we are wasting away, yet inwardly we are being renewed day by day. For our light and momentary troubles are achieving for us an eternal glory that far outweighs them all. So we fix our eyes not on what is seen, but on what is unseen. For what is seen is temporary, but what is unseen is eternal."*

What a paradigm shift!

From My Life to Yours

~What are you focusing on – the physical or spiritual side of things?

~ I encourage you to find a Bible verse that you can use to get you through the tough days. You can write it in your journal, or even on a note card to carry with you. Here are a few suggestions:
- ~ 2 Corinthians 4:16-18
- ~ Isaiah 57:1
- ~John 16:33
- ~Romans 4:18-25

Part Two

A Glimmer of Hope

July 23, 2009: Dad Squeezed My Hand

I have great news… I asked Dad to squeeze my hand & he looked at me and then about 15 seconds later he slowly gripped my hand!!! I've read that sometimes there is a delayed reaction to commands and that we need to wait long enough to give them time to respond. I am very encouraged! They are starting a medication stimulant tomorrow (Ritalin) to see if they can arouse him more. He also moved his eyes twice slightly to focus on me.

July 24, 2009: Dad's Next Facility

Today was mentally exhausting as we went through the ups and downs of deciding Dad's next facility placement. We visited several places, discussed options with case managers, health care providers, admissions specialists and the insurance company and finally have a peace about the decision.

Dad will be moved to a Barberton Sub Acute facility on Monday called Manor Care. He will be among friends and closer to home there.

From My Life to Yours

~ The journey that comes after a tragedy can be full of ups and downs. I encourage you to start a list of the "ups" that you can reflect on to encourage you during the downs.

July 25, 2009: Back to the Basics

I realized today that I need Jesus more than ever. Facing the tragedy of my dad's assault and coma has caused me to come back to the basics...my relationship with Jesus. If I don't keep my focus on Him, I am doomed.

I started a new devotional today called: "Jesus Calling" by Sarah Young. All I can say is POWERFUL! Just what I need each day to keep focused on what will keep me anchored during this difficult time.

From My Life to Yours

~What are you relying on during this time? Are you trying to survive on your own strength, or do you trust God to get you through?

~When you start to get weighed down, I encourage you to remember the words Paul wrote in 2 Corinthians (vs. 12:9-10) and then pray for God to give you His strength:

"But he said to me, 'My grace is sufficient for you, for my power is made perfect in weakness.' Therefore I will boast all the more gladly about my weaknesses, so that Christ's power may rest on me. That is why, for Christ's sake, I delight in weaknesses, in insults, in hardships, in persecutions, in difficulties. For when I am weak, then I am strong."

July 26, 2009: Fearing the Future

I am trying to live life "normally" by working and keeping up with my responsibilities. However, it's not always easy.

This weekend, I had to work at the hospital for the first time since Dad's assault. I usually work as a Physical Therapist in an outpatient clinic and just work on the weekends once a month. Well, this was my weekend to work.

My first patient of the day was a woman who is bed-ridden, has end stage dementia, is unable to follow commands and lays in bed in the fetal position most of the time. She lives in a nursing home and has a bed sore right now.

And as I started working with her, I was flooded with emotions thinking about my dad and picturing the possibility that he could be in a similar position someday. The doctors have told us from the beginning that the worst case scenario for Dad's recovery is that he could be in a vegetative state for the rest of his life.

I had to stop and refocus myself.

First of all, we still have 100% hope that Dad can completely recover. Second of all, I have sensed from God that I am not to picture and imagine these "doom and gloom" pictures of Dad's physical and cognitive abilities. It only opens me up to despair. Instead, what I am to picture is that Jesus is with Dad and taking care of him. And I don't have to worry because he is in good hands.

It reminds me of a section from the book, "The Shack" which is a fiction book, but depicts one man's journey of healing.

His name is MacKenzie or "Mack" and this is a conversation he has with Jesus. I will share a portion of the book with you below. [1]

> "Tell me what you're afraid of Mack." (Jesus)
>
> "Well, let me see. What am I afraid of?" began Mack. "Well I am afraid of looking like an idiot, I am afraid that you are making fun of me and that I will sink like a rock. I imagine that –"
>
> "Exactly," Jesus interrupted. "You imagine. Such a powerful ability, the imagination! That power alone makes you so like us. But without wisdom, imagination is a cruel taskmaster. If I may prove my case, do you think humans were designed to live in the present or the past or the future?"
>
> "Well," said Mack, hesitating, "I think the most obvious answer is that we were designed to live in the present. Is that wrong?"
>
> Jesus chuckled, "Relax Mack; this is not a test, it's a conversation. You are exactly correct, by the

way. But now tell me, where do you spend most of your time in your mind, in your imagination, in the present, in the past or in the future?"

Mack thought for a moment before answering. "I suppose I would have to say that I spend very little time in the present. For me, I spend a big piece in the past, but most of the rest of the time, I am trying to figure out the future."

"Not unlike most people. When I dwell with you, I do so in the present — I live in the present. Not the past, although much can be remembered and learned by looking back, but only for a visit not an extended stay. And for sure, I do not dwell in the future you visualize or imagine. Mack, do you realize that your imagination of the future, which is almost always dictated by fear of some kind, rarely, if ever, pictures me there with you?"

Again Mack stopped and thought. It was true.

He spent a lot of time fretting and worrying about the future, and in his imaginations it was usually pretty gloomy and depressing, if not outright horrible. And Jesus was also correct in saying that in Mack's imaginations of the future, God was always absent.

"Why do I do that?" asked Mack.

"It is your desperate attempt to get some control over something you can't. It is impossible for you to take power over the future because it isn't even real, nor will it ever be real. You try and play God, imagining the evil that you fear becoming reality, and then you try and make plans and contingencies to avoid what you fear…..

"So why do I have so much fear in my life?"

"Because you don't believe. You don't know that we love you. The person who lives by their fears will not find freedom in my love. I am not talking about rational fears regarding legitimate dangers, but imagined fears, and especially the projection of those into the future. To the degree that those fears have a place in your life, you neither believe I am good nor know deep in your heart that I love you. You sing about it, you talk about it, but you don't know it."

When I went back to the P.T. office to type my evaluation, I did end up crying. I allowed myself to feel the emotion of sadness and let it pass.

But, I don't need to be controlled by my fear of the future. Jesus is here with me and He is with Dad.

No matter what is ahead or what happens to Dad, I can rest knowing Jesus is here leading us and empowering us one step at a time. It's a daily battle to surrender the future to God (and sometimes a minute by minute battle) but the *only way* I will survive all the unknowns.

> *"There is no fear in love. But perfect love drives out fear, because fear has to do with punishment. The one who fears is not made perfect in love."*
> - 1 John 4:18

From My Life to Yours

~ Are you afraid for the future like I was? If so, I encourage you not to dwell on the unknown. Jesus once said: *"...do not worry about tomorrow, for tomorrow will worry about itself. Each day has enough trouble of its own."* (Matt. 6:34) When you start to imagine what might happen, remember His words of wisdom.

July 26, 2009: Tips for Caregivers

As we've been going through this crisis with my dad, I've reached out to several organizations for information to help us get through. Some of the information had tips for caregivers.

I've been pretty good at eating and sleeping, but over the last month I have been neglecting proper exercise. I haven't been motivated even though I knew it would help me. Well, today, I've finally gotten my jogging shoes on and went for a short jog. I am out of shape, but it sure felt good to "pound" the cement as a stress reliever. And I know that if I stay consistent with it, it will help me feel better.

Here were some other tips I recently read about:

"When you are a caregiver, it is important to take care of yourself so that you have something to give others. The following suggestions may help.

* Ask for help when you need it. Caregivers frequently try to handle everything alone. Expecting too much of yourself may add to the stress. Do not be afraid to ask for help. Find options for assistance like home healthcare or respite care.

* Set limits. There are only so many hours in the day and only so many things you can do. Some things can wait.

* Plan something to look forward to each day. Reward yourself for caring.

* Take time away from the person you are caring for. Taking an hour, a day, a weekend or a week away can do wonders to restore your emotional well being.

* Maintain contact with friends and family with whom you can discuss concerns or have fun.

* Take care of yourself. Caregivers are vulnerable to stress-related illnesses. If you have questions or concerns about your health, make an appointment with your physician. Tell your physician about your situation.

* Take time for exercise. Exercise increases stamina, lessens anxiety and depression, improves or maintains muscle tone and strength, and increases self confidence. These benefits make exercise a worthwhile use of your limited time.

* Learn relaxation techniques such as breathing exercises, meditation or progressive muscle relaxation.

* Join a support group. Support groups provide an opportunity to share problems and concerns. People with similar issues understand what you are feeling.

* Keep your sense of humor. Laughter is a great stress reducer because, for a moment, you are not thinking about your problems." [2]

From My Life to Yours

~Have you been neglecting any of the caregiver tips that I just mentioned? If so, set time aside as soon as possible to do one of the ones that you have been neglecting as soon as possible.

July 26, 2009: On the Road Again: Traveling Back to Akron

In a couple hours (after I shower and pack), I will head back to Akron to see my dad.

Tomorrow, I will attend a conference on Traumatic Brain Injury and hopefully learn information that will help us in making decisions on his care and rehab. I also hope to network with other therapists to use as a resource to ask questions along Dad's road to recovery. Pray that God would open the doors for me to connect with the right people tomorrow.

Dad is planning on being transferred to a new facility tomorrow as well. So, I will be there Tuesday to help get him settled, meet all his therapists and spend some time with him. Pray that this transition goes well and that Dad continues to make progress each day.

Tuesday afternoon, I'll return to Findlay so I can work Wednesday and Thursday. Then, I'll probably return to Akron Friday for the weekend.

Whew! A lot of driving and unfortunately CJ won't be able to come with me this week. But, I know that I will have my "Constant Companion" with me and that I'm never truly alone...

> *"God has said, 'Never will I leave you; never will I forsake you.' So we say with confidence, 'The Lord is my helper; I will not be afraid. What can man do to me?'"* Hebrews 13:5-6

July 26, 2009: When the Sun Shines

This is an entry from my mom, Gwen Ebner.

> "I had signed up for a golf outing to support new research for Crohn's disease. As I was traveling to the golf course, the skies let loose with a downpour. Would we be able to participate in this event? But before long the rain let up and we started to play. However, 30 minutes into the event it began to mist and the sky looked dreary

and gray. After awhile I found myself feeling cold, wet, and discouraged. "And why did I sign up for this", I said to myself a couple of times. For an hour the sky "spit at us" but finally, unexpectedly, the sun came out and the rain stopped. When I began to warm up, I took off my nylon jacket, my clothes dried out, and my spirits lifted. I felt hope and joy return.

Oh, how often life seems this way to me. Some 'rain' comes my way and I begin feeling discouraged. I wonder, 'why am I in this place.' But if I wait long enough, the sun comes out and I feel hope return. The "Son" warms my heart and reminds me that He is with me even in the storm and that I can trust and hope in Him…regardless of my feelings or circumstances. Oh, may I learn that lesson well and trust that truth, regardless if the rain is a mist or a downpour!"

From My Life to Yours

~ While the people and circumstances that surround us often bring us much encouragement, on occasion they won't be so encouraging. People get busy and the clouds roll in. It's important to remember that God is always with us. The next time you're feeling alone or weighed down by gloomy circumstances I encourage you to remember that God is with you.

July 26, 2009: At the Hospital With Dad

I was at the hospital earlier tonight with Dad...his eyes were open and he turned his head toward my voice several times. The aide said he seemed more active today moving his legs and I could see more spontaneous movement in both his arms and his legs. It's comforting to just be able to sit in the room with him again after being gone a couple days.

I showed a few pictures to Dad and he seemed to focus in on them. I updated him on the last few days and told him a few stories. He would be alert with his eyes open for a while and then he would close his eyes and rest for awhile.

I miss my dad.

I miss talking to him and connecting to him. This Wednesday will be one month since the assault. My emotions have been up and down today, ranging from sadness to grief to guilt to anger to fear. They say this is normal to have a flood of conflicting emotions in this part of the crisis response called "recoil." Normal or not, it's not very fun!

But, I am encouraged. Even since the last time I saw Dad two days ago, he is moving more and appears more alert. Each time I see him, I see small improvements and that is encouraging.

From My Life to Yours

~ Emotions are God's gift to us. The author of Ecclesiastes wrote that *"there is a time for everything, and a season for every activity under heaven"* (3:1). The point is that while it might not be any fun to experience conflicting emotions, it is okay to cry, to hurt, and to grieve. What it's not okay to do is let those emotions control you. So right now I encourage you to take the time to grieve, but also to cry out to God and put the situation and your emotions in His hands. Ask God to help you through this time, and to help you see even small improvements as encouragement.

~ If you haven't been adding to your list of "ups" take some time to read through it and add some more.

July 26, 2009: Praying for Grandpa Chuck

This is an entry from my sister, Stacey Reeder.

> "My husband, Brent and I have started a routine with our girls (Lauren-almost 4, and Allie-2) at bedtime that after our general prayers, we pray for Grandpa Chuck. Lauren has been the one primarily voicing these prayers, and they are so precious. Her prayers have included phrases such as:
>
> 'Thank you for Grandpa Chuck's boo-boo because we can pray for Grandpa Chuck.'
>
> 'We pray for Grandpa Chuck because he has a boo-boo on his brain.'

'We lift Grandpa Chuck to you and we ask for healing.'

'Grandpa Chuck needs a lot of help right now, and there is only one person who can help him–mommy.'

It just warms my heart to hear Lauren pray for my dad, and I know that God will honor her prayers.

Often times, I'm unsure how much Allie knows or understands about all of this. But, last night, after our normal bedtime prayers, we were starting to say good-night, and Allie said 'boo-boo…pawpaw.' She was letting us know that we needed to pray for Grandpa Chuck!"

From My Life to Yours

~ Are you spending time in prayer for the other people affected by the tragedy in your life? While it's important to trust God in our lives, it's also important to pray for the others in the same situation as well. I encourage you to take some time right now to lift up those around you in prayer. Thank God for being in control of their lives, and ask Him to watch over them and help them get through this difficult time.

July 27, 2009: A Few Highlights from Today

Today felt like a very long day with a lot jam packed into it. I went to a conference on traumatic brain injury today in Akron and also helped Dad get settled into his new facility. I'm just going to share a few highlights…

Dad's transfer seemed to go well to the Barberton SubAcute facility called Manor Care.

He seems a little more alert today and is moving his left shoulder more. His friend, Sheri Sanchez asked him to reach for her hand with his left arm and he lifted his arm slightly off the bed! I asked him to do it for me later and he repeated it two more times. Definitely encouraging progress.

The course I went to on brain injury gave me some good information and a couple contacts I can keep in touch with throughout Dad's recovery when I have questions.

The good news from the course is…prior to 2005, all research assumed that brain cell growth (neurons) did not occur in the adult brain, but there is now research to show otherwise. They call this neuroplasticity and say "neurons that fire together, wire together." There are still a lot of unknowns, but it offers those with brain injuries a lot of hope!

So, all in all, I am encouraged today! I will be here in Akron tomorrow and then head back to Findlay so I can return to work Wednesday and Thursday.

I have more to share about today, but that will have to wait until tomorrow…my bed is calling my name.

From My Life to Yours

~ Have you taken the time to be thankful for the technology, research, and just society that we live in during this difficult time? With resources such as cars, telephones and internet it's easier to communicate with those around us, which means when we need someone to talk to, they are only a phone call away. Today's medicine is far from perfect, but it's still 100% more efficient then it was only 10 short years ago. I encourage you to take some time right now to thank God for the advancements that you have found the most helpful.

July 28, 2009: The Tidal Wave of Emotions

Although yesterday was very encouraging for many reasons, I was also hit pretty hard with a tidal wave of emotions. And today, I feel like I'm experiencing the "emotional hangover!"

The TBI conference I went to was very good and I don't have any regrets about going at this time in my dad's recovery. But, emotionally it was hard to process all the information.

Punched in the Stomach

There was one point in the conference after hearing many stories and being refreshed on the functions of the brain that I felt as if I'd been "punched in the stomach." I then began to feel like I was going to get sick and vomit. Luckily, the instructor decided to take an early lunch.

The Emotions Tumbled Out...

I could barely make it to my truck before the sobs escaped. I started driving to lunch and then decided to just pull off in an isolated part of the parking lot. And I cried and cried. I felt so angry that this happened to my dad. I started screaming, "It's unfair!!" over and over while I was beating the truck seat.

I was grieving over the losses my dad might face and that our family might face. The thought even went through my mind that I'd rather him pass away peacefully than to live with any residual deficits. And then I felt guilt for thinking that.

Up and down my emotions swirled.

And then I decided to turn on my worship music. I found the song by Kim Hill, "You are still holy" and sat crying as I listened to it.

My Chevy Colorado Became a Sanctuary

I allowed myself to feel my emotions and let them pass through. As the song "You Alone" by Kim Hill started playing God brought back to my mind a story my mom had reminded me of the day before.

It's a story Corrie ten Boom shares (a Nazi concentration camp survivor). She says that when they would travel anywhere on the train when she was a little girl, her dad would keep their tickets. And then, at just the right time, as they were boarding the train, he would hand Corrie her ticket.

In the same way, I sensed God saying to me that He has my "ticket" right now. My "ticket" represents Dad's prognosis, outcome and the answers to all of this. And when I need these answers, He will give them to me at just the right time. Until then, I can trust Him with all the unknowns, the unanswered questions and the pain. I am in a waiting phase.

Strength Will Rise As We Wait Upon the Lord

Yep…you can guess it…this was the next song that came on my playlist.

Just as I was praying and journaling about waiting on God a song comes on to encourage me in that. Coincidence? I think not.

It reminded me of a verse that keeps recurring over the last month…

> *"Do you not know? Have you not heard? The LORD is the everlasting God, the Creator of the ends of the earth. He will not grow tired or weary, and his understanding no one can fathom. He gives strength to the weary and increases the power of the weak. Even youths grow tired and weary, and young men stumble and fall;* **but those who hope in the LORD will renew their strength.** *They will soar on wings like eagles; they will run and not grow weary, they will walk and not be faint."*
> Isaiah 40:28-31

Missing My Dad

I have had waves of missing my dad the last month. It comes and goes. Yesterday as I sat in my car, I didn't hear an audible voice, but below is what I sensed God saying to me as I was journaling...

> *"Shelley, I love you. I am your Heavenly Father. And I love you. I know that your earthly father isn't able to show his love for you right now, but I am able to. If you'll let me. It's hard because of the anger, hurt, and other emotions. But, realize I am not the author of pain or hurt or violence. What I created in the Garden of Eden was devoid of that. Heaven will be devoid of that. I know it's hard to understand and I don't expect you to. The big question you have is 'Why do I allow it?'*
>
> *Think of your two year old niece, Allie, trying to understand Calculus and Physics. No matter how much she tries, it just won't make sense to her yet. And the same is true for you. You can wrack your brain and think and analyze and study and discuss and still never figure it all out yet...on this side of heaven. Right now, what it boils down to is your view of me and if you trust me."*

I admit that I don't have all the answers. I'm convinced there are certain things I won't completely understand this side of heaven. But, as I sat in my truck a peace began to return to me.

Trusting the "Engineer"

And I thought of this quote from Corrie ten Boom...

"When a train goes through a tunnel, you don't throw away your ticket and jump off. You sit still and trust the engineer."

And in the same way, my train has just entered a dark tunnel. Instead of throwing away my ticket and jumping off, I am choosing to sit still and trust the "Engineer."

From My Life to Yours

~ Set some time aside to worship God. While the things we are going through are far from easy, it's important to remember that He is still holy. I encourage you to say a prayer and/or turn on some worship music and spend some time worshiping our Creator, then agree to wait upon His timing and trust Him with this tragedy.

July 28, 2009: Dad Stood on His Feet in Therapy Today!

Believe it or not....Dad actually stood up on his feet in physical therapy today! It was so good to see him sitting on the edge of the bed and actually standing for the first time since his assault almost a month ago.

He required the assistance of two therapists, but they said he did actually use his leg muscles to help when standing. He's been kicking his legs A LOT in bed, so it doesn't surprise me that he was able to use his legs in standing.

The therapist said it really can make a huge difference in their progress once they start bearing weight through their legs because of all the other things that benefit from being in that position.

So, it's great that they are able to start standing right away with Dad! They showed me a special device they have that they can use with patients like Dad where they have a platform for his feet, support in front of his shins and a table to support his arms. Then, they put a support around his waist and the machine assists him to stand up. Over time, they gradually take away the supports so that he can learn to stand on his own again. They will evaluate him with it tomorrow. Very cool.

I really like his therapists. His P.T. is Bernadette (Bernie) and his P.T.A. is Donna. Bernie is young, enthusiastic, full of energy and I could tell that after she heard Dad's story, she is very motivated to help him in every way possible. Donna has over 32 years of experience with 11 years of experience specifically with patients with brain injuries like Dad at Edwin Shaw rehab. So, he's got some great people working with him that are willing to do whatever it takes to help get him better.

The last few days, Dad has been laying with his arms curled up most of the time. However, as he was sitting on the edge of the bed with the therapists, they worked on putting weight through his arms and he actually relaxed his arms. They said this is a very good sign.

Speech Therapy

Dad also had a speech therapy evaluation today. Since his assault, he has keep his teeth clenched together most of the time and the nurses haven't had much success with getting him to open his mouth.

However, today when the Speech Therapist was working with him, he opened his mouth to her command several times and we felt like we witnessed a small miracle!

Compassionate, Caring and Relational Staff

What we like best about the Manor Care staff is how compassionate, caring and relational they are. They really seem to care about their patients and have demonstrated such compassion to Dad already. Not only are they skilled in the therapy he needs, but they truly seem to care! That really makes all the difference.

Back to Findlay to Work

I am now back in Findlay and tomorrow my alarm will go off at 4:30am so that I can be at work seeing patients at 6am! I will work Wednesday and Thursday and then drive back to Barberton Thursday night. Stacey will be coming for the weekend and bringing the girls so that will be a blessing. We are praying for her as she'll be driving 9 hrs with two little ones.

Encouragement and Progress

Today was a day of encouragement and progress. I'm so glad I could be there for his first therapy sessions and that God allowed me to see the progress Dad is making.

I give God all the glory for the healing taking place with Dad and am thankful for all of the people who are standing with us during this time, and for their prayers.

From My Life to Yours

~ I encourage you to thank those who are helping you through this time. Whether you write a thank you note, express your thankfulness face-to-face, or even just call them on the phone doesn't matter. Why not make a list of all the people who have helped you during this time, even just a little bit, and make a point of expressing your gratitude to them?

Part Three

A Foundation of Hope

July 29, 2009: Faith That Can Move Mountains

As I've been praying for Dad's physical healing, I have to admit that I have struggled to have faith. I have a strong personal faith and do believe in God's power to do what's humanly impossible, including healing Dad's physical body. But I also have medical knowledge with my job as a Physical Therapist and know the "facts" behind his diagnosis and injury.

To be honest, this has caused a struggle within me to believe that supernatural healing is possible.

You see, Dad has been diagnosed with diffuse axonal injury (severe brain injury) and that is the primary reason he has been in a coma. But, according to the CT scan, he also has a hematoma in the frontal lobe of his brain. It's there and according to doctors, the damage done by that hematoma is irreversible. And yet, I believe that God still performs miracles. Therefore, I struggle with the reality that he has the severe brain injury and hematoma and the belief that God can still heal him.

My Crisis of Belief

So, do I believe what the "experts" tell me or do I believe what God tells me?

Now, don't get me wrong. I do believe in listening to your doctor's advice. But, I don't want to allow them to discourage me and give up all hope. I want to believe that it is possible for God to heal my dad in such a way that a repeat CT scan would show no evidence of that hematoma.

And if God chooses to heal my dad in that way, God will receive all the glory.

"What is impossible with man is possible with God." Luke 18:27

I have prayed that Dad's healing would happen in such a way that only God can receive the glory.

My mom sent me encouragement the other day on listening to other people's words and advice. She was reading Nehemiah chapter 6 where people outside of Judah were saying words to discourage Nehemiah from rebuilding the walls of the city.

He didn't listen but chose to keep listening to what God was telling him. She encouraged me by saying, *"Don't let anyone discourage you right now, Shelley, with their words…keep listening to God and stay faithful to what He's given you to do – rebuilding the walls!"*

However, God's Answer May Be Different Than Mine

The other struggle I have right now is that God's answer for Dad's healing may be different that what I want or expect.

And so I struggle with how to "pray in faith believing" and yet not have an expectation that God will answer my prayer in a certain way, so that I don't set myself up to be disappointed and disillusioned if He chooses to answer my prayer differently than what I expect and want.

My Year of Faith

Even before this happened to my dad, I remember telling someone that the past several years have been intense years of healing in my life, whereas I felt as if this year was going to be a "year of faith."

At that time, I had no clue how deeply my faith would be tested this year with my dad's assault and resulting coma!

A few months ago, I remember wrestling through some of these issues surrounding faith. Yesterday I re-read one of my journal entries from May 22nd, 2009 that describes some insight I believe God gave me.

At the time, we were trying to sell our house so we could downsize, pay off our loans faster and eventually phase me out of my job. This would then allow CJ and I to travel together in ministry full time and possibly start a family.

A lot of changes, but the first step was selling our house. Or so we thought. And so we decided to pray that we would sell our house for our asking price and that the buyer would pay the closing costs. Here is my journal entry from that day a few months ago…

"Lord, I was feeling recently that I don't want to have a minimalist attitude that says we will just 'survive' and break even on selling our house. I want to believe You and that in Your power You can work a miracle and bring someone that will pay our asking price and closing costs.

I struggle though with faith to believe that can happen because you may choose to provide for us financially in other ways. So, I sensed You saying to me that I can have faith that You can provide a buyer who will pay our asking price and pay closing costs and if You do provide that person...YOU will receive ALL the glory.

Because there is no way in this economy and this housing market that would ever happen otherwise.

However, I need to trust you to provide for us. And if it isn't through selling this house at our asking price and not paying closing costs then you will provide financially for us another way. This way I don't get disillusioned if you don't "answer" my prayer that I prayed "in faith" the way I expected you to.

I think so many times I have seen faith as a way to control You, to be bossy and tell You what to do (the way I want it done). And yet that is just the result of my pride. Faith is really a belief in Your power and then a surrender and trust in You to do it YOUR way even if it isn't my timing or how I want it done.

I want to have the faith to believe in Your power to provide a buyer quickly and yet trust you to provide a buyer (the right buyer) for us even if it takes longer to sell our house.

It really is a surrendering of my control. And it comes down to trusting You.

Help me, Lord to believe in Your power and to trust Your to provide everything we need. More than anything I want to bring You glory! I want you to inspire people to believe You through what they see You doing in our lives. Just like I have been inspired through the example of other people's lives."

That day, I had a paradigm shift in my view of faith. And in my journal I wrote out this summary:

Surrender in Faith	vs.	**Control/Bossiness**
Trusting God to do it		Telling God what to do
(Humility)		(Pride)

How This Relates to Dad

So how does this relate to Dad? Well, in the same way, I can either choose to surrender Dad's prognosis and final outcome completely to God trusting Him to do it, even if it isn't in my timing and the way I want OR I can try to control God through my prayers and in a bossy attitude tell God what He needs to do for my dad.

See the difference? It really boils down to control vs. surrender.

And for today, I choose surrender.

I may have to surrender it over and over to God in any given day, but that's okay. There is a learning curve. And I have a great Teacher!

> *"I tell you the truth, if you have faith as small as a mustard seed, you can say to this mountain, 'Move from here to there' and it will move. Nothing will be impossible for you."* Matthew 17:20

From My Life to Yours

~ Are you trying to control your situation, or are you trusting God with your situation? Today, I encourage you to surrender to God, put your faith in Him and trust Him with the past and the future.

July 29, 2009: Heart of Gratitude

There are many things I am thankful for today.

> I am thankful for the great progress we have seen in Dad the last couple days. It's wonderful to see him moving his legs, sitting up and following a few commands.
>
> I am thankful for the summer days and sunshine where I am able to enjoy the outdoors.
>
> I am thankful for the family that has opened up their home to me when I am in Akron...even giving me a key to come and go as I need. Thank you!
>
> I am thankful for our friends who dropped off packed lunches for the next couple of days.
>
> I am thankful for all the cards people have sent as encouragement.
>
> I am thankful for the gift cards for gas and food people have sent to us to use when we visit Dad...thank you!
>
> I am thankful for my husband who gives the best hugs in the world!

I am thankful for a mom, who is also one of my best friends and is there for me when I need to talk and process all that is going on.

I am thankful for my sister who is one of the few people who truly understands what I'm going through.

I am thankful for my nieces, Lauren and Allie, who bring so much joy to my life.

I am thankful for a good job that provides for us financially during this time.

I am thankful for two working vehicles that take us back and forth to Akron.

It truly has been amazing to see the body of Christ at work. Many of you have showed your support for us through sending cards, e-mails, food, money or prayers.

We have truly been blessed by all of those around us, and now, by you… thank you!!

"I thank my God every time I remember you." Philippians 1:3

July 30, 2009: The Jesus Prayer from Terry Bohannon

This is from my cousin Terry Bohannon (his mom Linnea is my dad's sister). I asked him if I could share it as an encouragement to all…

"There is an old prayer that I like praying, it's short and direct. It's called the Jesus prayer, it's "Lord Jesus Christ, Son of God, have mercy on me, a sinner."

When I start to feel overwhelmed with anxiety or passion, the prayer brings me to a quick focus so that I no longer feel overwhelmed. It also keeps me humble, because when I pray the words I am reminded of how much I do not deserve Christ's grace and how dependent I am on his mercy."

From My Life to Yours

~ Over the course of this book, I have encouraged you to be thankful for many things, advancements in technology and research, and for those around you, but today, I just encourage you to make a list of general things that you are thankful for. Write it down so that you can continue to add to it.

July 31, 2009: Great Progress in Therapy

Yesterday Dad had an amazing day in therapy! He sat up on the edge of the bed and held his head up on his own...Auburn said Dad even had a small smile on his face! He also stood with support for 20 minutes! The staff gathered to cheer him on!

I got a message from his Physical Therapist last night that she stayed late to work him out again. We are thankful for all the progress and the people God is providing to help Dad!

July 31, 2009: Speech Therapy

Stacey and I were both able to attend Dad's speech therapy session this morning, thanks to Katie for watching the girls (Katie is the daughter of my dad's former Captain at the Salvation Army in Akron).

Dad's Speech Therapist, Katherine, deflated his trach today to see how he tolerated breathing out of his normal airway and had him hooked up to a monitor to evaluate his oxygen levels the entire session. I didn't time it, but he was able to maintain normal levels of oxygen saturation the entire session! Therefore, the Speech Therapist said she would recommend to the doctor to progress Dad to the next step with his trach, which is a speaking valve. This would be put over his trach to allow him to vocalize (right now he can't) and he would have to cough up any secretions on his own.

This will be introduced gradually to make sure he can tolerate it. It is good news that he is ready for the next step!

She also uses frozen lemon ice to help stimulate Dad's oral motor responses. She said that it's a combination of the cold and the sour taste that helps promote the response. Dad was opening his mouth for her and swallowing as needed. She said he was using his cheek and lip muscles well and showed us certain exercises we can do with him over the weekend.

His Speech Therapist is also trying to develop a communication method that Dad can use with us. Whether it is two blinks for yes and one blink for no, one finger for yes and two fingers for no or turn his head to the right for yes and to the left for no…it will be a major breakthrough for him to be able to communicate with us.

We sense that he can hear us and can understand. If so, it will give him a sense of empowerment to be able to communicate with us! Please pray that a means of communication can be established with him soon.

I watched Lauren and Allie in the afternoon so Stacey could be with Dad and observe his physical therapy session.

We colored, made up stories, watched a movie, painted nails, had a tea party and played at the park. Whew…we had a fun time! What joy they bring into my life!

From My Life to Yours

"A happy heart makes the face cheerful, but heartache crushes the spirit." Proverbs 15:13

~ When walking through a tragedy, it can be tempting to let it consume your life. Today, I encourage you to get out and do something - just for the fun of it. It's important to remember that even after a tragedy, life goes on – and it's important to have joy in our lives.

August 1, 2009: Lauren's Visit and a Smile

This is another entry from my sister, Stacey.

> "Today, after much thought and prayer, I decided to take Lauren to see Grandpa Chuck.
>
> Auburn and I decided that it would be best for dad to be in his chair in the courtyard for Lauren's visit, to help him look as natural as possible.
>
> Once we got there, Lauren was a bit apprehensive and unsure of it all. But, then she started asking curiosity questions (i.e., 'Why does he have a red bracelet on?' 'What is that?'–pointing to his catheter bag, etc.), and making observations about what she was seeing (i.e., that dad's look on his face was very serious, his arm moving, etc.).
>
> Soon, she began dancing, jumping, and playing, and appeared to be fairly comfortable. She didn't talk much to him, although she told him a couple 'knock, knock' jokes.
>
> While we were there, dad was awake (although he would close his eyes at times and quickly re-open them), and was fairly active. He moved around quite a bit...moving his head, arms, legs, and back

(as if re-positioning himself). And, he appeared to be looking at us at various times.

The COOLEST thing for me from the whole visit was when we were about to go. I leaned down, put my arm around dad and said, 'It was SO good to see you today, dad.' And, immediately, the corners of his mouth began moving upward into a SMILE!!! He even smiled so big he showed off his toothless grin!

It completely made my day. I felt like he was saying, 'It was so good to see you, too.'

Afterwards, when we were going back to the house, I asked Lauren what it was like to see Grandpa Chuck, and she said, 'Awesome.' That was good for me to hear."

August 2, 2009: New Movements

Every new movement that Dad makes gives us hope that he is continuing to heal and recover. Yesterday, Stacey took Lauren to visit Dad for the first time and when they were getting ready to leave, he smiled a big open mouth smile for the first time!!

Later, after Lauren's birthday party, Auburn returned to Manor Care to see Dad and he was straightening and bending his left elbow. Previously, he only lifted his left shoulder to the side. More new movements!! She also saw him lift his head up toward the ceiling for the first time.

He has been able to move his head side to side, but this was the first time he lifted his head up to the ceiling.

Smiles, elbow movement, partial head nodding....all encouraging signs that Dad's body is continuing to heal...one day at a time!

From My Life to Yours

~ Hebrews 3:13 says: *"But encourage one another daily, as long as it is called Today, so that none of you may be hardened by sin's deceitfulness."* So today, I encourage you to think of a way that you can encourage someone else. Whether it's someone who is walking through the tragedy in your life with you, or someone going through something completely different, find a way that you can encourage them.

~ I also encourage you to review the list of "ups" that you wrote down and add any more that you can think of to them.

August 2, 2009: Rebuilding After a Storm

I feel more at peace today. I realized yesterday that I have spent every waking moment thinking about Dad or being with him. Therefore, I took yesterday off from visiting

Dad and instead spent the day watching the girls so that Stacey could be with him. I needed that mental break from it all and my nieces bring so much joy into my life!

Last night CJ came for Lauren's b-day party and we were together for the first time in a while. It was so good to talk and process with him and spend some time re-connecting with each other. Much needed! We've spent so much time apart these last few weeks.

I need to find balance in all of this. I started to get sick with a cold this weekend and I think it was my body telling me I need to take care of myself too during this time. I was able to get over 9 hours of sleep on Friday night which felt really good! I've also been taking some of Dad's "Get Well Soon" supplements from Arbonne…so even in a coma Dad is helping take care of me.

Finding Safety in the Storm

Today I felt like I needed safety from the storm swirling in my life right now. I sensed God say to me that He is here with me and that I can find safety and refuge in Him…even when I feel like everything around me is uncertain and feels unsafe.

> *"The LORD is my rock, my fortress and my deliverer; my God is my rock, in whom I take refuge. He is my shield and the horn of my salvation, my stronghold."* Psalm 18:2

I got a picture of what that "safe refuge" looks like for me. There may be times when I have to go out in the storm and get wet and cold. But I know that God is always with me. He will never leave me or forsake me. And whenever I need rest, our safe place is waiting for us. I pictured that safe refuge as a warm inviting cave where I am protected from the storms. God offers me warmth by the fire to dry off and food for my soul. He says, "Come to me all who are weary and heavy laden and I will give you rest for your souls."

He walks with me. He doesn't stay behind in the cave. He will be with me to give me the strength and wisdom I need to navigate this storm. Storms come and go and I can't predict when they will come.

This is a storm that has entered my life. I wasn't expecting or planning my dad to be assaulted resulting in a coma and a severe brain injury. But, now I have to deal with it. Kind of like floods, wild fires, hurricanes and earthquakes are unexpected disasters that leave behind so much damage.

I feel like my life is in rubble again. It feels as if my heart is broken and hurting.

Rebuilding After a "Storm"

This is what I sensed God saying to me in my journal today:

"Shelley, you may feel like your life is in rubble again, but realize that I am able to 'restore what the locusts have eaten' and I am the Ultimate Rebuilder of hearts and lives. As we work together at 'rebuilding the walls' of your life, there will be a greater and deeper beauty seen in you than was evident before. I am able to bring good out of any situation...I am about healing and restoring the brokenhearted. Beloved, your heart has been broken, but as we rebuild and restore the brokenness within you, there will be a beauty that far exceeds anything you could have

imagined before. Trust me. Hold on to my hand as we walk through this storm together. Come take shelter with me and find refuge in me. And surrender your broken heart to me. I am the Healer and Restorer of broken hearts."

And so, today I found that peaceful place again. That safe refuge. I'm not sure how long this storm will rage, but I do know that I can always find safety in Him in the midst of it all. And I am given the hope of a promise today. The promise of rebuilding after the storm....the rebuilding of my broken heart.

> *"He heals the broken hearted and binds up their wounds."* Psalm 147:3

> *"He has sent me to bind up the broken hearted."* Isaiah 61:1

From My Life to Yours

~ What do you feel like God is telling you today? I encourage you to look for something He might be trying to teach you during this time of healing.

Part Four

Day by Day

August 3, 2009: Progress and Changes

Today was another day of progress, but also a day of changes.

A Private Room...Finally!!

Over the last week, Dad has been at Manor Care in Barberton. We were told that a private room would be available last Friday, however, the person occupying that room decided to stay longer. This was very disappointing to us.

First and foremost, we have been told that a person recovering from a brain injury needs quiet and rest. We have had doctors and nurses tell us that even the background noise of a TV or overhead lights can force the brain to use all of its energy to filter this stimulation instead of using that energy for healing. Therefore, having a roommate is not ideal for Dad's diagnosis.

And even though Dad's roommate is a nice guy, he is also hard of hearing. Therefore, when the health care workers come in to talk to him, they talk VERY loud! Not usually good for dad. The other negative is the extra germs in the room from his roommate's cough. I'm sure it is not ideal to be in the same room with someone who is coughing germs into the air.

Therefore, due to these concerns of having a roommate (as well as safety concerns and trach care), we were seriously considering transferring Dad to a new facility.

However, Dad's friend Sherri Sanchez decided to talk to the family in the private room about Dad's situation. And after talking with them, they decided to leave today which allows Dad to be in a private room tonight with his own bathroom. Woo Hoo!! One problem solved!

Physical Therapy Changes

We were disappointed to find out that Dad's Physical Therapist was laid off as of today. However, the Physical Therapy Assistant working with Dad is now taking over his case and she has 11 years experience working with brain injuries at Edwin Shaw Rehab Center. Auburn was very impressed with her work today. She talked calmly and quietly to not overstimulate him. She has a different approach than the other therapist, but Dad seemed to respond to her.

Physical Therapy Progress

The physical therapist stood Dad with the external support of a device. She then lowered him into a squat and you won't believe it...but, Dad then proceeded to perform seven squats in standing on command! She was going to do passive exercises on his legs, but said she didn't need to; his muscles are already working and active.

She also worked on weight shifting in standing...bumping his hips from one side to another. She said it's still too early to work on walking even though Dad seemed to want to advance his legs.

They also put electric stimulation on Dad's neck/shoulder area earlier in the day. This is done to stimulate the nerve endings. Later, he was lifting his head and shoulders off the bed as if he wanted to sit up. This is a new movement. While he was doing this, Auburn took his hands and he easily sat up on the edge of the bed.

Safety Concerns and Issues

The Speech Therapist is still working proactively with Dad to wean him from the trach. The sooner the better.

Today, Auburn saw Dad reaching for his trach and wrapping his hand around it. Then, he gently unwrapped his hand from the trach and lowered it again. The safety concern is that he may try to grab and pull out his trach. As people recover from a coma and become more active, they can also become agitated. Therefore, the doctors and nurses in the hospital warned us that he might try to pull out his trach. The Occupational Therapist has tried different things to deal with this, but really hasn't found a good solution yet.

They did say that you can use a big mitt over the person's hands, but it is also considered a restraint, which skilled nursing facilities in Ohio aren't allowed to use. Therefore, we are still working with them to find a way to get the mitts. He wouldn't need them all the time, only when he is alone in the room.

As Dad has gotten more active, the other safety issue is his increased risk for falls. Since they aren't able to use restraints, they can't use bed rails. Therefore, they have an order for his bed to stay low to the ground with matting surrounding it. For a few days they hired someone to come and sit with him during the night, but they informed us today that they will no longer be able to do this for us. However, with him being transferred to a private room, it will open up the opportunity for Auburn to stay the night with him more often. However, she is still looking for people in the area that would be willing to volunteer and come and sit with him at different times to help give her a break.

We are praying that God will protect Dad regarding these safety issues and that God will help us to not worry.

We are praying that we will discern when we need to be proactive and when we need to trust Him.

Summary

So, today was full of updates. To summarize:

Dad will be staying at Manor Care in Barberton for now. We will keep our options open and if needed have researched other facilities.

He is being transferred to a private room today

His physical therapist who will schedule his therapy from 3-4 pm so that he can sit up in a wheelchair for visitors from 5-6pm.

He squatted 7 times with support, on command!

They started electrical stimulation to his neck and shoulders which seemed to help him sit up on the edge of the bed easier.

They are working on weaning him from the trach. The sooner the better.

We are still working on the safety issues. I have come to realize that there will most likely be safety issues throughout Dad's healing and recovery due to the brain injury. We are praying that God will protect him and help us not to worry!

Whew! A lot to share today.... I am very thankful for the continued prayers and support!

From My Life to Yours

~ Some days are busier than others and it always helps me to process things by writing them down, so I encourage you to do that as well. Write down what's been going on lately, both good and bad. Be sure to note your feelings about each situation, and then spend time praying about situations, and thanking God for breakthroughs and progressions.

August 4, 2009: Encouragement for Today

My encouragement for today came from my mom. I am thankful to have her not only as my mom, but also as my close friend and confidant. Here are a couple things she passed along to me today.

Faith vs. Knowledge

"Faith is not necessary when you know how things are going to work out – that's knowledge. It's in the time of unknowing that having faith is what sees you through to the other side. Faith is what gives you strength.

Faith is that light in your heart that keeps on shining even when it's all darkness outside. Now is the time to keep that faith alive!"

And It Came to Pass

My mom sent me this e-mail:

> In my one year bible we are starting on Job. Charles Stanley made this comment about Job 1:
>
> "There is a limit to adversity. It will come to an end. One woman quoted to me a favorite Bible phrase of hers: "and it came to pass." She said, "Just think – it came to pass. It didn't come to stay!"
>
> Remember that today's troubles are just that: today's troubles. A season of trouble is just that: a season of trouble. Crises pass. Circumstances change. Situations evolve. God works in and through adversity to bring it to an end, according to His timetable."
>
> I thought that was helpful today as I read it and thought I'd pass it on.
>
> MOM

Thanks Mom for that encouragement today!

> *"May our Lord Jesus Christ himself and God our Father, who loved us and by his grace gave us eternal encouragement and good hope, encourage your hearts and strengthen you in every good deed and word."* 2 Thessalonians 2:16-17

From My Life to Yours

~ I've mentioned this before, but it's important to remember that even if we think it would be easier if this tragedy was the end of the world, it's not. Life goes on. While my mom encouraged me with the above verse and quotes, I want to encourage you with a quote from the book of 2 Corinthians (12:9-10) *But he said to me, "My grace is sufficient for you, for my power is made perfect in weakness." Therefore I will boast all the more gladly about my weaknesses, so that Christ's power may rest on me. That is why, for Christ's sake, I delight in weaknesses, in insults, in hardships, in persecutions, in difficulties. For when I am weak, then I am strong.* - Let Christ be your strength.

August 5, 2009: More Movement

As Dad gains more and more movement, he requires more supervision to keep him safe. Auburn was called in last night at 3 am to help keep Dad in his bed. He gets very active, partially sits up, tries to get out of bed, and pushes himself sideways. Auburn takes these opportunities to work with his body–help him sit, let him roll to his stomach, encourage him to push this, move that. She said during the day he tried to get out of bed at least three times. It looks like they are going to put another mat around his bed for additional padding.

This is a season of <u>extreme</u> high-maintenance (picture a 145 pound newborn with very strong legs). We are praying for those caring for Dad that we would stay healthy and not wear ourselves down. Also we're praying for peace of mind, that we wouldn't be controlled with worry and anxiety about Dad's safety.

On the Road Again…

Time to pack my bags again! I will be traveling to Barberton/Akron area tomorrow after work and staying through Tuesday to help Auburn by taking shifts with Dad. CJ will be able to be with me over the weekend, so that is a relief. Already this seems like such a burden, but we are hoping that this high maintenance stage will not last long.

Conference with Staff

We have been researching all the different options available for keeping Dad safe and keeping us sane during this time.

We have scheduled a conference with the staff at Manor Care for Friday at 1pm. It will be a chance for us all to discuss and work together on Dad's behalf. We are praying for this time to be effective and productive. We also have been asking for prayer for the staff that works with Dad everyday. Praying that God gives them wisdom and compassion for Dad and that God would use them to minister healing to Dad's mind, body and soul.

Other Updates

We are hoping to get a local doctor on Dad's case to make certain processes go faster and to oversee his progress. In his current situation, the doctor is not available much and therefore not as proactive as we'd like on weaning Dad from his trach.

We have good news...they removed the catheter today! Dad had been extremely uncomfortable with it for many days and has likely has developed an infection. For some reason, it is taking nearly a week to get the infection diagnosed and treated, hence the potential need for his own doctor. Also, we want to get much more aggressive on the removal of his trach. He doesn't need it and remains at much higher risk of complications like pneumonia with it in. We also have to get the trach out to think about getting the feeding tube out.

"Is He Still in a Coma?"

I've had several people ask if Dad is still in a coma. It's a fairly difficult question to answer.

Most people think someone is either in a coma or isn't. But, it's not that simple. The physical therapist working with Dad said she would rate him as an "emerging" level 3 on the Rancho Los Amigos Coma Scale. There are different stages as you come out of a coma.

Dad does open his eyes, but he is not consistently following commands or speaking yet.

You can see more explanation at these links: http://www.northeastcenter.com/rancho_los_amigos.htm and http://www.braininjury.com/recovery.html

August 6, 2009: Be Still and Know

This entry is from my sister, Stacey.

> "This morning I was studying Psalm 46:10, *"Be still and know that I am God,"* and was challenged and encouraged by what I learned.
>
> I've always thought of the phrase of *"Be still"* to mean not to move or act, but I had more insight after looking up the Hebrew for "still." I found meanings such as...."relax," "sink down," "to let go," "to be quiet," and "withdraw."
>
> I got the picture of relaxing my body, letting it sink down into the chair, and seeing my arm fall and releasing whatever was in my hand.
>
> Too often I hold on so tight to whatever I may be facing, trying to figure it out on my own, trying to make sense of it, trying to control it.
>
> So, to be still and know that He is God is to let go of what I am holding on to and allowing, or rather, trusting God to be the sovereign, all-powerful God...the Creator of the universe.
>
> So in times of worry or distress about my dad or the future, I can visualize releasing my burden while trusting that God has a plan in all of this....and that's where I will find peace."

From My Life to Yours

~ Real life isn't always as simple as black and white. The process of recovery isn't all fun and games. Life is hard. No matter where we are in our road to recovery, it's important to remember that God works all things together for the good of those that love Him (Romans 8:28), and even when we walk through the valley of the shadow of death, He is with us (Psalm 23:4). So I encourage you to say a prayer asking God to get you through this. Ask Him for the strength that you, and those around you, need to get through this, and for Him to continually remind you that He is with you, and things are getting better. Be still and know that He is God.

August 7, 2009: Spending the Day with Dad

CJ and I arrived last night in Barberton to be here for the next few days. We were able to see Dad and spend a couple hours with him while he rested last night.

A Few Heartwarming Moments

We were able to have a few heartwarming moments with Dad over the last 24 hours. One was this morning when I was kneeling at the side of his bed, he lifted his left arm and wrapped it around me like he was giving me a hug.

He did this three different times and once actually pulled me in, closer to him!

It was the first time I sensed my dad reaching out to show me love since his assault.

It was also great to see Dad smile. We had him outside in the courtyard and I was telling him about a cardinal I had seen. There was a bird house in front of us that said "The Tribe." CJ then said, "Dad, I don't think you'd see any Cardinals landing on this birdhouse…it says 'The Tribe!'" Dad immediately broke into a big smile like he understood.

Later, I told him one of the knock knock jokes from Lauren's book we got her for her birthday. After I said the punch line he broke out into a big smile. Now, that's my dad!!

A Day in the Life of Chuck Sandstrom…

Today I spent 13 hours with Dad all together…it was definitely a jam-packed day.

It started out with occupational therapy. I discussed our concerns about getting some type of splint or brace for his hands. Last night when I first arrived, his left hand was on his trach and his right hand was on his feeding tube. He still doesn't have a real strong grip on either hand, but probably enough to try to pull out his trach or feeding tube. Since they aren't able to use restraints in a skilled nursing facility, the occupational therapist had to get creative. He came up with the idea of these palm protectors, which would still keep his hands from gripping, but aren't considered a restraint. So far, it seems like it is working and helps relieve us from worry.

Another of our concerns has been his risk for falling out of bed due to his increased mobility. They are keeping his bed low to the ground (the lowest setting is 13 inches from the floor) and have placed mats around his bed. They are also using a wedge on one side of him. We asked for another wedge for the other side and that seems to help as well. They changed his mattress today to a scoop mattress which is in the shape of a U with higher sides. All of these things will help with safety to prevent falls for Dad. However, when Dad is awake, he continues to be a "mover and a shaker." He moves a lot! Therefore, it will still be important for someone to be in the room with him. We are going to try to find volunteers that are willing to stay with Dad to give Auburn a break.

He did start an antibiotic today to treat his UTI. We also were able to get aerosol treatments started today. They are breathing treatments to help with his trach. He will now be getting these on a regular basis.

Due to the increased risks associated with having the trach, we would really like to see him weaned off of it as soon as he can tolerate.

We found out today that he should be starting to work with a speaking valve on Monday and the respiratory therapist will come on Monday to assess him as well for a cap for his trach. They said it depends on how well he tolerates everything how fast it can be removed. At least we are seeing progress in the right direction!

Family Conference

So, it was great to begin to have some of our concerns addressed and positive action taken today. We had a family conference with the staff this afternoon and it went very well. They listened to our concerns and helped us brainstorm solutions. It was especially good to talk to his doctor. He seemed genuinely concerned and willing to help in whatever way. We cleared up a few misunderstandings we had and now feel better about the care Dad is receiving at Manor Care. They are truly a compassionate staff and we can tell they genuinely care about Dad. And for that, we are most grateful.

We have especially been impressed with their rehab staff. From speech therapy, occupational therapy and physical therapy, they have all done an outstanding job with Dad.

In physical therapy today, Dad worked on opposite, reciprocal movements of his arms and legs on a recumbent bike. It took quite a bit of effort and support to get him in place, but once he was there, he was able to do it! The longest he biked continuously was for 45 seconds. He still has a short attention span due to the brain injury, so he should continue to improve both with his endurance and his attention span with time and practice.

Finally Some Rest!

He finally got some rest today. It seemed like he didn't sleep much at all the past 10 days, but he did sleep last night and then slept another 5 hours today. It's good to finally see him resting and getting some deep sleep. We think it may be a combination of addressing the UTI and the pain he probably had with it as well as backing off his Ritalin. We are thankful to see him resting deeply again.

Another Move?

Auburn has been in contact with the insurance nurse case manager and is still considering a move to another facility. There is a possibility he could be moved within the next few days, but we haven't heard anything for sure. One of the reasons we may move him is due to insurance. Manor Care is out of network which creates several issues with insurance and may create problems if he needs to stay in a skilled nursing facility longer than 30 days.

Also, the place he could possibly move would have 7 days of therapy vs. 5 days (Dad doesn't get therapy on the weekends at Manor Care) as well as "net beds" which would provide more safety for him during this period of increased mobility. A "net bed" basically looks like a large playpen and helps prevent falls for patients like my dad.

We'll let you know when and if he ends up moving. But, for now, we are content to stay at Manor Care.

A Burden Lifted

Today was a day that I could feel a burden lifted. After a lot of worrying this week from a distance about Dad's safety, it was good to see some positive steps taken. I feel that it was an answer to our prayers.

The last few days I have been meditating on 2 Timothy 1:7 using the Amplified version. *"For God did not give us a spirit of timidity (of cowardice, of craven and cringing and fawning fear), but [He has given us a spirit of power and of love and of calm and well-balanced mind and discipline and self-control."*

I'm continuing to pray for a spirit of calm and well-balanced mind!!

One other thing that has helped me the last couple days is to listen to John Eldredge's "Daily Prayer" in my car. It's not "magic" or a formula, but does help me to set my mind back on Christ and his power in the midst of my circumstances.

You can access those at:
http://www.ransomedheart.com/node/636

From My Life to Yours

~ We've talked a lot about writing down the encouraging things that happen, but today, I want to encourage you to make a list of concerns that you have. What are some of the things that you have been worrying about or that have been taking up a good deal of your thoughts during this time of healing? These are things that you can pray about and trust God to work out for His glory.

August 8, 2009: Starting to Get My Dad Back

I feel like I'm starting to get my dad back. He seems to be responding to us more and more.

Yesterday, I felt led to pray for Dad when CJ and I were with him. We held his hands forming a circle and each prayed. I watched Dad and during the prayer, he had a tear rolling down his cheek that he then wiped away with his left hand. I believe he was with us and was touched by our support and prayers.

Smiles, Smiles and More Smiles

Something else that has changed today is that Dad has started to smile more often. Since Dad doesn't get therapy on the weekends, I decided to do some with him. I stretched his arms like occupational therapy does and worked on his mouth movements and following commands like speech therapy does. Then, we did some music therapy. I decided to turn on some of his favorite music…Chicago. He tapped his toes and moved his head to the music. I said something like, "Dad we're playing some of your favorite music, it looks like you are enjoying it! I can see you tapping your toes!" He then smiled really big.

When CJ returned from his trail run, he said, "Dad, I hear this woman has been working you out pretty good!" And again came Dad's big smile!

Later, his sister Rebecca and cousin Shirley called. I put them on speaker phone and they started talking to him. Almost immediately, he broke out into a big smile!

Just a Normal Saturday Afternoon

This afternoon, they sat him up in his wheelchair and we decided to turn on the golf tournament and allow Dad to watch Tiger Woods play. As we positioned his chair toward the TV in his room, he propped up his legs on the edge of the bed. He looked so comfortable! And it looked like he was just hanging out in his recliner to watch golf with us on a lazy Saturday afternoon like we've done so many times before. It actually felt kind of "normal" for a little while.

Starting to Communicate

Today Dad started to communicate with us. I asked him to raise his hand if he needed something and he raised it high. For several different occasions and appropriately!

I also began to work with him on mouthing the words yes and no. Once he started to do both yes and no, I asked him a couple questions. I asked him if his name is Chuck and he mouthed "yes." I asked him if his wife is Auburn and he mouthed "yes."

It was such a breakthrough to begin to communicate with him! I can't wait for him to try the speaking valve in speech therapy.

Following Commands

Today Dad began following commands better. And when I was getting ready to leave, I asked him to give me a "high 5" and he did with his left hand! He had kissed me on the cheek earlier in the evening and so Auburn asked him for a kiss. He puckered up and gave her a kiss. It was the first time he kissed her like that on command!

I really feel like I'm starting to get my dad back!

From My Life to Yours

A cheerful heart is good medicine, but a crushed spirit dries up the bones. Proverbs 17:22

~ When was the last time you were cheerful? Do you have some favorite music that is fun to dance to that you could turn on? What about just hanging out and enjoying time with friends and family?

August 10, 2009: Lots of Time with Dad

I just finished 28 hours at the nursing home with Dad. Yep... 28 hours straight. I didn't leave. Not even to eat...brought my cooler of food instead so I could eat my meals there. Didn't sleep either. Well, maybe a cat nap or two. But, the important part is that Dad stayed safe while Auburn went out of town overnight last minute!

Anyone who knows me knows that I do NOT do all-nighters and never have. Never did stay up all night at sleepovers, never did all night study vigils in college and only did it this time out of necessity...for my dad's safety.

Actually, I have spent over 50 hours with Dad the last four days! Wow!

You might wonder why we have to be in the room with him when there are nurses and aides to take care of him. Well, it's pretty complicated. As he gets more mobile and emerges out of the coma, his safety concerns are very real. And because of the strict rules about nursing homes NOT using restraints, our options are very limited. There are times you literally can not leave him for even a minute because he can find a way to wiggle off the bed or get his hand to the trach. Like I've said before…he is a mover and a shaker. And that's why we have been providing round the clock care.

Therefore, for my peace of mind and Dad's safety, it was well worth it.

Update on Speech Therapy

Dad should get started on the speaking valve in Speech Therapy tomorrow and if all goes well and he tolerates it, they may be able to remove the trach within a week. We found out he has to have his trach out to qualify for a net bed at Edwin Shaw Rehab. So, for now, he will stay at Manor Care and work hard this week on breathing on his own!

From My Life to Yours

~ The process of healing after a tragedy takes a lot of work. Can you think of the steps that are going to be required in your own process of healing, whether it's forgiving someone, re-learning to be happy, or learning/teaching someone to talk or walk again, write it down so that you can better track your healing process.

August 11, 2009: Battling Resentment

I don't know about you, but I believe in a spiritual battle between good and evil. And I feel like I have been in an intense battle this weekend, especially with my enemy called Resentment.

Ephesians 6:11-13 says,

> *"Put on the full armor of God so that you can take your stand against the devil's schemes. For our struggle is not against flesh and blood, but against the rulers, against the authorities, against the powers of this dark world and against* **the spiritual forces of evil** *in the heavenly realms. Therefore put on the full armor of God, so that when the day of evil comes, you may be able to stand your ground, and after you have done everything, to stand."*

I woke up last night around 2am and couldn't fall back to sleep. My mind was swirling with thoughts. And Resentment was starting to win. And really, I had a good logical case and many good reasons to feel resentful. It was easy to feel justified in my Resentment.

But, I felt Resentment's grip becoming tighter. The picture I got was of Resentment being a type of "poison" for my spirit and my soul. I wrote in my journal, *"I feel like I have a poison trying to kill me. The poison of Resentment."*

So, at 2am I was in need of a drink of water…badly. I had some bottled water in my truck and wandered outside in the dark for some water. And I ended up sitting on the front porch looking at the sky…the moon and clouds and stars. It all reminded me of God's creation and His greatness and how I have NOT been relying on Him much this week. Instead I've been relying on human wisdom. And have been more vulnerable to spiritual attack.

I went back to sleep and when I woke up I felt like a load had been supernaturally lifted from my shoulders.

I needed to refocus

Kind of like putting on the correct prescription of glasses, my world became "fuzzy" this week and I needed to set my eyes back on Christ and His power to help me through all of this.

Instead of focusing on what I've lost, I need to focus on what I have.

Instead of giving in to Resentment and Anger, I need to ask God to empower me to show grace to imperfect people…especially since I am one of them! And remembering that *"hurt people hurt people."* I will really need God's empowerment for this on because I know that I don't have it on my own.

I may not like my circumstances, but there are certain things I have no control over and cannot change no matter how hard I try. Therefore, I realized this morning that I need to reach a place of acceptance in order to move on (still working on this one.) This was a big one for me, realizing that acceptance is different than approval. Although I don't approve of certain things that have happened (and never will), I can still come to a place of acceptance of my current circumstances.

Can I trust that God will work good out of bad?

Can I trust God with all of this? Can I trust Him to protect me and help guide me as I make decisions?

I am so imperfect and make mistakes every day in the things I say and the decisions I make. I am so prone to giving into feelings of anger, bitterness, resentment, fear, selfishness and self pity. I need a supernatural power and infilling of the Holy Spirit more than ever.

And am I ever grateful for new starts…for God's forgiveness of my mistakes. I am grateful for a new day!

> *"Because of the LORD's great love we are not consumed, for his compassions never fail.* **They are new every morning**; *great is your faithfulness. I say to myself, "The LORD is my portion; therefore I will wait for him."* Lamentations 3:24-26

Have Your Way Lord…

Not my will, but Yours Be done. ~Jesus

From My Life to Yours

~ I encourage you to answer the questions that I asked myself in this chapter:

Can I trust that God will work good out of bad?

Can I trust God with all of this? Can I trust Him to protect me and help guide me as I make decisions?

~ Next, say a prayer letting God know that you either trust Him or need help trusting Him, and ask for His will to be done.

August 11, 2009: Back in Findlay

After spending 5 days in the Barberton/Akron area and many hours at Dad's bedside in the nursing home, it's time for me to return home. For now. To reality. To my job.

Dad Started the Speaking Valve!

We continue to gain encouragement each day with small baby steps. Dad started the speaking valve today in Speech and actually hummed for the first time! Aunt Rebecca (Dad's sister visiting from Houston) and I were able to talk to the Respiratory Therapist and she has a protocol for helping get Dad off the trach. First he will try the speaking valve and then be transitioned to a cap.

It's all a very gradual process to make sure he can tolerate it well because the last thing they want to do is remove the trach too early and have to intubate him again.

Best case scenario would be in one week IF he is able to cough on command to clear his airway. Please pray for this process of weaning from the trach to go smoothly and for him to be able to cough on command.

Physical Therapy

He seems to be advancing faster physically than he is cognitively, but we see small progress in each area every day. He worked hard in physical therapy today. It's amazing how quickly the simplest things tire him out. They were working with him laying on his stomach on a wedge picking up bean bags and putting them in a container. They said it was not only working him physically, but cognitively as well because it was a 2-step command. He was able to do it, but it took a lot of patience and waiting for him to figure out what he needs to do next. This is normal as the brain is healing.

He also started walking to the bathroom today with the help of Auburn and one of the aides.

Hugs and Kisses

Dad definitely seems to respond to family. When I got there today, he kept giving me hugs with his left arm (his stronger arm) over and over. He also gave me several kisses on the cheek. Right now, the two commands he responds consistently to is... "Dad, give me a high five" and "Dad, give me a kiss."

Please pray for continued healing on his brain, especially in the area of his cognition and following commands. The physical therapist says he follows commands ~40% of the time.

Encouragement for Today

I heard two stories of people who sustained severe brain injuries that are now functioning well. That gives me hope! One is from a post from family friend who posted on our blog.

The other story was from the physical therapy aide. Her uncle sustained a brain injury from a car accident and was in a coma 6 weeks. He is now driving again and functioning well.

What we almost always hear is that it takes a long time. We have wanted a miraculous healing and still praying for that, but also realize that God could heal him little by little over several years. Either way, I was very encouraged to hear these stories of recovery!

August 12, 2009: Sacrifices Made

Many people have made sacrifices since Dad's assault. Some big, some small. Some life changing, some not.

One of the small sacrifices CJ and I have made during this time is that we have had to cancel two vacations. Doesn't sound like a lot to most, but it was a pretty big deal to us for multiple reasons that I won't go into right now.

However, we have had a weekend trip planned to the Upper Peninsula in Michigan for a while. And we leave tomorrow! We will be staying in a cottage on Lake Superior for three nights and will celebrate our 11th wedding anniversary while we're there. CJ will run in one of his trail races for the Trophy Series and this time I'll be there to cheer him on.

I'm so thankful for the small blessings. Blessings like a weekend away.

In our eyes it seemed as if our vacation was "taken" from us. But, now we have been "given" this weekend to enjoy. It reminds me of the song *"Blessed Be the Name"* based on Job 1:21…He gives and takes away.

> *"The LORD gave, and the LORD has taken away; Blessed be the name of the LORD."* Job 1:21b (NKJV)

August 13, 2009: It Feels Like a Miracle

Today Dad spoke his first words since he was first assaulted and went into a coma six weeks ago!!! WHOOOO HOOOO!!! There are not words to express how thankful we are for this breakthrough.

It feels like a miracle.

Aunt Rebecca was there with him during his speech therapy today and gave me the report. They are gradually increasing the time he wears the speaking valve again and allowed him to wear it for two hours.

She said "Good Morning" to Dad and he replied "Good Morning." He was also counting (not sure how high!). The speech therapist asked him his name and he responded "Chuck Sandstrom" three times!! He also tried to sing Jesus Loves Me and Happy Birthday.

Aunt Rebecca says he hasn't lost his sense of humor because the speech therapist asked him if he had a sister (with his sister Rebecca sitting right next to him) and he said, "no." Then she asked him if he was kidding and he said, "Yes!" and smiled real big. Later, he was slipping in his chair and they commented, "You're slipping in your chair." And he said, "Oh well." About a dozen staff members at Manor Care were there crying and cheering him on!

We are overjoyed with his progress and thank you all for your prayers! God is answering your prayers and amazing us with the progress Dad is making everyday.

All I want to do is give thanks and praise to the Lord today!!

[1] Praise the LORD.
Praise God in his sanctuary;
praise him in his mighty heavens.

[2] Praise him for his acts of power;
praise him for his surpassing greatness.

[3] Praise him with the sounding of the trumpet,
praise him with the harp and lyre,

[4] Praise him with tambourine and dancing,
praise him with the strings and flute,

[5] Praise him with the clash of cymbals,
praise him with resounding cymbals.

[6] Let everything that has breath praise the LORD.
Praise the LORD.

Psalm 150

From My Life to Yours

~ Count your blessings and spend some time thanking God for each one. This would be a good time to read through your list of "ups" but also to thank God for things unrelated to your tragedy.

August 17, 2009: The Love of a Father

One thing I can say for sure is that my dad loves me. As an adult, my emotional relationship with my dad was restored. Some of my fondest memories are from Wednesday nights at Stonebridge Church of God when we would meet one on one to pray together. He took time to spend with me and show me his love.

We met faithfully together until CJ and I left for Belize and I believe these times created a strong bond between us that lasts today.

Now, as my dad emerges from the coma, our relationship is different. Instead of him taking care of me, I am helping take care of him. For many weeks, he has been unable to show any affection or love to me due to the coma. However, as he is now emerging out of the coma he has begun to shower me with hugs and kisses on the cheek!

The love of a Father

As I've walked through this life changing journey the last few weeks, music has ministered to my soul. One song that has meant a lot to me is called, "Father Me" by Paul Oakley. It is hard for me to listen to this song and not cry. Several times as I've listened to the song, I have felt God whisper to me,

"Shelley, even though your father is unable to show his love and support for you right now, your Heavenly Father is able. I am here for you. And I love you. I am proud of you."

Here is this encouraging song, "Father Me" and the lyrics:

> *You have loved me with such perfect love*
> *Fathered me with such a tender touch*
> *Your faithfulness surrounds my soul*
> *Your mercy lifts my head*
> *How could I repay all you have done?*
>
> *Father me, faithful Father*
> *Father me, no-one else could ever be*
> *The perfect Father God to me*
>
> *You now clothe me with your righteousness*
> *Hide me in the shadow of your wings*
> *And even in my darkest days*
> *Your light will guide my way*
> *Hallelujah to the King of grace*[3]

From My Life to Yours

~ No matter what happens, it's important to remember that God loves us. I encourage you to take some time right now and thank God for His love as well as spend a few moments worshiping and praising Him for His faithfulness.

August 17, 2009: Visiting Hours Update

Here is an update on visiting hours from Auburn.

Do stop by to see Chuck. ***We are no longer limiting the hours.***

However, here is what visitors should know.

Chuck is frequently asleep and wakes easily, so tip-toe. Please don't wake him up.

Please leave a note in our guest book for Chuck.

When Chuck is awake and aware, speak to him rather than around or over him, touch him, tell him of things he would be familiar with and keep your sentences simple. Keep your voice at a normal, not loud, volume.

When Chuck is awake but not sociable or responsive, you might just sit with him quietly.

Keep visits short. Make way for therapists, aides, nurses or other activities going on in the small room.

Help keep Chuck safe. If you notice he's active and in danger of coming out of the bed or chair or of pulling off some medical equipment, please stop him. There is also a call button clipped to his bed should you need assistance.

Chuck can be quite sociable and responsive now, but his attention span is short, so don't take it personally if he looks at you intently one moment then turns away the next.

His smile is priceless, but be prepared to see him minus his two front teeth. Can be a bit startling.

I am often in the room and too tired to be very charming or coherent. Ignore me.

We appreciate your love and concern for Chuck.

From My Life to Yours

~ Have you thought about making a list of things that the people around you should know during your time of healing? How can they help you and what should they be aware of? Take some time now to write one out.

Part Five

Hope Breaks Through

August 19, 2009: Hearing Dad Talk for the First Time

I was with Dad today and heard him talk and say my name for the first time in 7 weeks! He was smiling and laughing at jokes appropriately which warmed my heart…he seems to still have "Chuck" in him…the Chuck that everyone knows and loves.

Jim Betts from the Salvation Army was visiting this morning and as Dad was standing up from his chair with Auburn's help, Jim joked with Dad about practicing his "Fred Astaire" moves. Dad got the joke, looked over at Jim and smiled real big.

Even the staff enjoys being around him, some stopping by just to visit. Last night a nurse and aide were standing him up and the nurse said "Okay Chuck, let's stand up on the count of three" and before she even said one he stood up. She jokingly laughed and said, "Okay, then. THREE!!" He looked over at her and smiled real big. He does stuff like that all the time. Staff has said things like, "I can see he has kindness in his eyes," "He is so wonderful," "Chuck is great."

Even after a severe brain injury, he is still drawing people in with his charisma!

Dad also talked to Stacey on speaker phone which made her day! Not only is his brain healing, but his mouth and tongue muscles are regaining strength as well. Therefore, he sometimes struggles for words and has difficulty pronouncing certain words. His voice sounds lower and different through the speaking valve but it is definitely music to our ears to hear him talking!!

In and Out of the Fog

Someone described emerging from a coma and recovering from a brain injury like being in a fog. You come out for moments here and there. I like thinking of it like that. Because there are moments of "clarity" where Dad is really with us and then there are moments that he seems to be in the "fog" and not responding as consistently.

Today, he was reading staff's name tags as well as the wording on one of his frames! So he can see and read...yeah!

He's also able to recognize people in pictures. I went to Wal-Mart tonight to have more pictures printed off. I was able to get a few pictures from his childhood (thanks to Heather posting them on Facebook), pictures from my childhood and recent pictures. All in all, there will be over 100 new pictures to help trigger his memories.

Hair Cut

Dad finally got his hair cut yesterday. He's looking good! He usually keeps his hair cut short and it had grown pretty long in 7 weeks! Ever since he started moving his left arm, he's tended to reach up and rub his head. I've often wondered if he was thinking, "Wow...my hair is getting long!"

Possible Transfer to Edwin Shaw

Now that Dad has progressed so well with his speech and cognition, he is being re-evaluated for a possible transfer to Edwin Shaw for intensive rehab. They will have a meeting tomorrow morning to decide if he qualifies, and if he does they will most likely transfer him tomorrow.

At Edwin Shaw they have an entire floor dedicated to brain injuries and are known for their work with patients like Dad. He will receive three hours of rehab when he's there. Lots of hard work, but at the end of his time there he should be ready to come home!

Prayers...

We are continuing to pray for Dad's cognitive and physical development...I believe we are seeing answers to prayers everyday and give God all the glory for Dad's amazing progress!

As Dad becomes more aware of his condition and the long road of rehab ahead of him, we're also praying for him emotionally and spiritually. We pray that God would provide the encouragement and motivation not only he needs, but that we all need to persevere.

Cap Finally Arrives

After getting two different caps for Dad's trach that didn't fit, we were very happy to see that the right size finally came in today. This is the next step in Dad getting weaned from the trach with the final goal of having it removed altogether. When Dad is wearing the cap, he is breathing completely on his own. They did a 30 minute trial today and his oxygen saturation levels stayed in the high 90's (which is very good, 100% is the best). They haven't given us a time frame but it could be within the next 1-2 weeks that he could have the trach removed depending on how he does. Also, he can't have his feeding tube removed until the trach is removed, so we're grateful he is moving on to the next step with his trach!

From My Life to Yours

~ What are you praying for? I encourage you to write down the things you are praying for in your journal. Are you praying for something physical like a cap for a trach, or something spiritual like encouragement and motivation? Whatever it is you need, write it down, then bow your head and ask God to provide it.

August 20, 2009: Resistance Verses Routine

Dad did really well today following commands in speech therapy, the best I've ever seen him...earning himself an "A+" for today!! He also did weight training in OT for his shoulders and grip strength and really worked hard tiring himself out (a good tired)!

He slept almost 4 hours and then worked out some more in PT. He has definitely improved in his sitting balance and his ability to sit up from the laying down position.

He also worked on walking with weights on his legs to help him with proprioception (where his body is in space). He still tends to lean backward a lot when walking and requires the support of two people. He did more reading today and picture recognition. He also worked on counting.

Dad is able to give one word answers to questions and follow commands pretty well. However, he has started initiating conversation more often and it is still pretty hard to understand what he's saying. This can be frustrating for him and for us as we try to figure out what he's desperately trying to tell us. Please pray that his speech and communication continue to improve and that we get better at understanding what he is saying.

Edwin Shaw Update

Someone is going to come on-site tomorrow to evaluate Dad for Edwin Shaw for intensive rehab. If they think he is ready for it, he could be transferred as soon as this weekend. We'll keep you updated.

August 21, 2009: Last Day of Therapy at Manor Care

We found out today that Dad will be transferring to Edwin Shaw for intensive rehab on Monday. And since Manor Care doesn't do therapy on the weekends, today was Dad's last day with the rehab staff at Manor Care that we have all grown to love and appreciate. Therefore, we took some pictures and video to remember them by.

I have one story to share with you from his therapy today. In speech therapy Dad was finishing sentences with a word (and did very well, by the way).

For example "You eat soup with a …" "Spoon." Well, he finished this sentence, "The children make too much…" with the word "Money" and began laughing, not just smiling, but laughing!! It was too funny and he had the whole therapy room smiling and laughing with him.

From My Life to Yours

~ Sometimes the road to recovery has chapters, when one ends another one begins. Can you think back through your recovery process and identify some of the different chapters? I encourage you to take some time to write them out. You can be as simple or as detailed as you want and just make an outline of your personal recover process.

August 21, 2009: The Greater Impact Dad is Having

One of the staff members that helps clean Dad's room was talking with me today. She said she works part time and it had been a week since she last worked. But she had heard about the amazing progress Dad is making. She said he's the "talk of the building" with all the other staff as they follow his progress.

I mentioned something about the miracles we are seeing each day. She said she hadn't seen any "miracles" for a while and had kind of given up believing. But, she said after seeing the progress Dad has made in the last month, she thinks she believes in miracles again!

She said, "I know that I only clean his room, but in doing that, I feel a part of something so much bigger, so much greater." I could sense a renewed sense of purpose in her as she talked.

God is at work and we thank Him for the miracles we see every day. And for allowing us to be a part of something so much bigger, so much greater!

> *"What is impossible with men is possible with God."* Luke 18:27

> Jesus said, *"I tell you the truth, anyone who has faith in me will do what I have been doing. He will do even* **greater things** *than these, because I am going to the Father. And I will do whatever you ask in my name, so that the Son may bring glory to the Father."* John 14:12-13

From My Life to Yours

~ Times of tragedy can be a great test of faith. How is your faith holding up during this time? Do you still believe in miracles? What about your witness for Christ? How's that holding up? I encourage you to take some time right now to write down the answers to those questions and to pray about those two things.

August 24, 2009: Dad Finally Made it to Edwin Shaw!

Well, Dad finally made it to Edwin Shaw Rehab. From the very beginning we have heard about Edwin Shaw and heard about their reputation for helping patients with brain injuries. We were told that what put Edwin Shaw "on the map" and made them well known was their work with brain injuries…they even have an entire floor dedicated to brain injuries. Dad is in good hands.

And he is also now in a net bed which will help ensure his safety as he continues to get more mobile.

But, it will be hard.

I'm a Physical Therapist and I know rehab. It will be tough! They say he will get 3 intensive hours of rehab every day. They will push him to progress. And I believe that Dad will step up to the challenges and the hard work that lay before him! Anyone that knows Dad knows he's determined. Once he sets his mind to do something, he'll do it. And I think he'll rise to the challenge once again.

We've been told that insurance could approve anywhere from 14 to 30 days at Edwin Shaw…then he will go home! It's hard to believe that within a month he could be home. Wow!

We are praying for these next days as he (and Auburn) learn all they need to learn before they go home together. That Dad would continue to heal emotionally, spiritually, physically and cognitively. That he would be an inspiration for others and a light for Jesus at Edwin Shaw as he has been at Manor Care. We'll miss everyone at

Manor Care, but are thankful to be moving on to the next step!

Go Dad Go!!

We're behind you every step of the way! And we love you!

August 24, 2009: Fill My Cup, Lord

Emilie Barnes shares this poem in her book *Fill My Cup, Lord* and I thought I would share it with you.

Fill my cup, Lord.
I hold it up to you with outstretched hands,
My heart parched and thirsty for your living water.

Fill my cup with your love, Lord.
Help me to feel your hands holding mine,
feel your arms around me, feel your love empowering me.
Fill me with quietness and encouragement and trust.
Help me to live for you when trials, difficulties,
and storms hit me and those I love so deeply.
Help me not to give up when giving up seems easier.
Help me to trust you when I don't feel like trusting anymore.
When I know pain, fill my cup with prayer.
Teach me the secrets of service and surrender.

Fill my cup, Lord. I lift it up to you.
Lift me up to do your will with love and sacrifice,
Never forgetting what you sacrificed for me-
Your Son.
My Messiah.
My Lord Jesus Christ.

Help me, Lord, to accept where I am now.
Help me to know I'm not stuck forever in my circumstances.
Help me remember that the windows do open
and that fresh breezes do blow in
and that living water forever flows
and that those who ask receive.
I'm asking, now, Lord.
I'm holding my cup in my hands,
And I'm asking you to fill it . . . with you.

And when my cup springs a leak,
As earthen vessels are prone to do.
Then I'll just have to ask again,
Trusting in your love
To fill me again . . .

Amen[4]

From My Life to Yours

~ Right now, I just encourage you to cry out to God and ask Him to fill your cup!

August 26, 2009: Quick Update

It sounds like Dad had a great day today!

In physical therapy he walked the length of the parallel bars with little assistance and stepped up and down on platforms the second round.

He walked the length of the therapy room twice with help & using a walker. Also, both his doctors were thrilled today with his level of responsiveness and plan to get the trach out in the next 48 hours!

Stacey and the girls are there to visit and I'll be in Akron tomorrow evening after work and plan to stay the weekend!

August 28, 2009: Edwin Shaw

Dad is doing great at Edwin Shaw Rehab Hospital. We're thrilled that he is in a net bed to keep him safe! Also, we have great news…his trach was removed yesterday! His swallowing is improving, but the Speech Therapist says it is still a little slow. They will keep working on his swallowing and next week the doctor will order a modified barium swallowing test. If Dad does well with the swallowing test, he will then start eating food as recommended by the speech therapist. The last thing he has left in him is the feeding tube. They are still giving him nutrition through it until he is able to advance to eating on his own.

Dad's Contagious Laughter

I have to tell you that Dad is making the best out of all of this. I think I laughed more today spending the day with Dad in his therapy sessions than I normally do. He still has a quick wit that gets us laughing! Today the Speech

Therapist was showing him pictures and asked him to identify a picture of a dog. She was pointing to the dog and asked him what it was. Dad said quickly and confidently, "NOSE!" and started laughing. Well, she was pointing to the nose of the dog, so technically he was right…and we all started laughing with him. He still has his signature laugh that he is so well known for and it is also very contagious…thanks Dad for brightening my day.

Here are a few pictures and videos from my visit with Dad today at Edwin Shaw.

Edwin Shaw Rehab Hospital

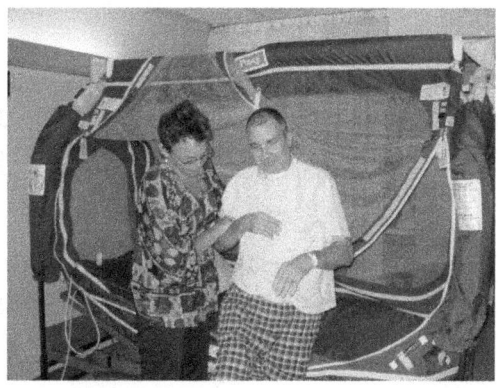

Dad & Auburn in front of his "net bed"

From My Life to Yours

~ I don't know where you are in the midst of tragedy, but there is always hope. I'm experiencing some amazing "ups" but even if you aren't, I encourage you to read through and add to your list of "ups" if possible right now. Each tragedy is different, and has a different road to recovery, but no matter what happens, there is light at the end of the tunnel.

August 30, 2009: Weekend with Dad

I spent this weekend in Akron/Barberton area visiting Dad at Edwin Shaw.

Family Visit

Stacey and her girls (Lauren and Allie) were also visiting this weekend. It was so fun to be able to see them and have some bonding time with my favorite 2 year old and my favorite 4 year old!

Mom and her husband Chet also came to visit on Saturday as well as Maw-Maw and Paw-Paw and our friend Homer Lentz. Homer took this group photo of us below.

Haircut

Stacey was able to save Dad some money by cutting his hair for him today since they charge extra for haircuts. Afterwards, he looked in the mirror and said, "Looks good!"

Singing with Grandpa Chuck

Today Stacey and I spent some time with Dad before we all left to go our separate ways. We were going over the days of the week with Dad and Lauren asked, "Is it okay if I sing the days of the week song for Grandpa Chuck?" We said yes and she started singing. Before she finished, Dad was singing with her! I could tell he remembered the song and the tune. Of course, his singing was not the same as before, but it was good to see him trying. We proceeded to sing other songs he might remember….the ABC's, Zaccheus was a wee little man, Row Row Row Your Boat and others…and he chimed in from time to time with us! How heart warming to see Lauren leading us in singing together with Dad.

Progress Each Day

Dad is now out of the coma and showing progress every day. He continues to amaze us at what he can do. For example, yesterday he stood next to the pool table with minimal support and was actually shooting balls into the pocket using a pool stick! I think he could beat me at a game of pool right now.

However, the most difficult aspect of his recovery continues to be his communication. From what we can tell, he seems to fully understand what is going on around him. He can answer simple yes or no questions and with simple one or two word replies, but has difficulty expressing himself when he initiates conversation. He may get out part of what he wants to say, "I am grateful for..." however the rest often comes out garbled. He often laughs at himself when this happens and rarely shows agitation, for which we are all thankful. Speaking and communication have always been one of Dad's strengths and so you can understand how this might be difficult for him to be limited in this area.

The doctor did say that the area of his brain most affected by the bleeding (left parietal/frontal) would tend to impact his ability to communicate. As we pray for Dad, we continue to pray for his ability to communicate and express himself to improve.

I Love You Dad...

For the last couple of months I have hugged my dad and told him "I love you, Dad." For a long time I got no response. Then, I started getting a left handed hug and kisses on the cheek. And today was the first time he verbally responded back to me, "I love you." It is really good to hear my dad say those words again to me. Even as he is recovering from a severe TBI, he is finding ways to show his love for us.

August 30, 2009: Overcome Evil with Good

Tonight I was going through a bible study and the topic was about overcoming evil with good. It was hard to hear, but a good reminder for me. Definitely not easy for me, but possible through God's empowerment.

> *Do not repay evil with evil or insult with insult, but with blessing, because to this you were called so that you may inherit a blessing.* 1 Peter 3:9

> *Do not be overcome with evil, but overcome evil with good.* Romans 12: 21

> *Do not take revenge, my friends, but leave room for God's wrath, for it is written: 'It is mine to avenge; I will repay,' says the Lord. On the contrary: If your enemy is hungry, feed him; if he is thirsty, give him something to drink. In doing this, you will heap burning coals on his head.* Romans 12:19-20

> *Bless those who persecute you, bless and do not curse.* Romans 12:14

> *Dear friend, do not imitate what is evil but what is good. Anyone who does what is good is from God. Anyone who does what is evil has not seen God.* 3 John 11

> *When a man's ways are pleasing to the LORD, He makes even his enemies live at peace with him.*
> Proverbs 16:7

From My Life to Yours

Be self-controlled and alert. Your enemy the devil prowls around like a roaring lion looking for someone to devour.
1 Peter 5:8

~ Tragedy is most often brought on by the evils of this world – evils that Satan would love to devour you. Are you letting that evil overcome you, or are you (with God's help) overcoming it with good? Take some time right now to both journal and pray about your battle with evil.

September 3, 2009: Update on "Walking and Talking"

Walking: Dad continues to show progress! Monday, physical therapy had Dad taking long walks down the hall using a wheeled walker. Dad tended to veer and get tangled up in his feet, so Auburn told her how little support he needed in the room for short walks to and from the chair. They proceeded to ditch the walker and strode up one end of a long… hall and back, just lightly guiding him at his elbows. The PT nearly cried & said, "Oh my gosh, you're going to be our poster child!" Bye-bye walker.

Talking: He also had a great conversation with his sister Linnea on the phone the other day. The best "talking" he's done for awhile.

September 4, 2009: Re-Learning Everyday Tasks

Dad continues to re-learn simple everyday tasks. Auburn says, *"Chuck leaned over yesterday on his own and tied his shoe. He stooped down, picked up some trash from the floor and tossed it in the wastebasket. After he brushed his teeth, he leaned down under the faucet, got water into his mouth, swished and spit it out. All the normal, automatic stuff seems to come spontaneously including Chuck's inclination to walk briskly rather than slowly."*

Eating and Drinking

The doctor has decided to wait until next week to do the modified barium swallowing test. Dad's swallowing is still a little slower than they'd like to see. Please pray for his swallowing to improve so that he can start the process of introducing eating and drinking again.

Balance in Walking

Dad is also walking better, but is still too unbalanced to walk on his own. Pray for his balance to improve and his ability to know when it is safe for him to move on his own and when it is not.

God as our refuge

And most importantly, pray for his spirit. Pray that he would find his refuge and hope in Christ during this time of rehab.

I was reading Psalm 31 today and it really resonated with what I'm going through right now.

*^{1} **In you, O LORD, I have taken refuge**;*
let me never be put to shame;
deliver me in your righteousness.

^{2} Turn your ear to me,
come quickly to my rescue;
be my rock of refuge,
a strong fortress to save me.

*^{3} Since **you are my rock and my fortress**,*
for the sake of your name lead and guide me.

*^{4} **Free me from the trap that is set for me,***
for you are my refuge.

*^{5} **Into your hands I commit my spirit**;*
redeem me, O LORD, the God of truth.

^{6} I hate those who cling to worthless idols;
I trust in the LORD.

^{7} I will be glad and rejoice in your love,
for you saw my affliction
and knew the anguish of my soul.

^{8} You have not handed me over to the enemy
but have set my feet in a spacious place.

⁹ *Be merciful to me, O LORD, for I am in distress;*
my eyes grow weak with sorrow,
my soul and my body with grief.

¹⁰ *My life is consumed by anguish*
and my years by groaning;
my strength fails because of my affliction,
and my bones grow weak.

¹¹ *Because of all my enemies,*
I am the utter contempt of my neighbors;
I am a dread to my friends—
those who see me on the street flee from me.

¹² *I am forgotten by them as though I were dead;*
I have become like broken pottery.

¹³ *For I hear the slander of many;*
there is terror on every side;
they conspire against me
and plot to take my life.

¹⁴ ***But I trust in you, O LORD;***
I say, "You are my God."

¹⁵ ***My times are in your hands;***
deliver me from my enemies
and from those who pursue me.

¹⁶ ***Let your face shine on your servant;***
save me in your unfailing love.

¹⁷ *Let me not be put to shame, O LORD,*
for I have cried out to you;
but let the wicked be put to shame
and lie silent in the grave.

[18] *Let their lying lips be silenced,
for with pride and contempt
they speak arrogantly against the righteous.*

[19] *How great is your goodness,
which you have stored up for those who fear you,
which you bestow in the sight of men
on those who take refuge in you.*

[20] **In the shelter of your presence you hide them**
from the intrigues of men;
in your dwelling you keep them safe
from accusing tongues.

[21] **Praise be to the LORD,
for he showed his wonderful love to me**
when I was in a besieged city.

[22] *In my alarm I said,
"I am cut off from your sight!"
Yet you heard my cry for mercy
when I called to you for help.*

[23] *Love the LORD, all his saints!
The LORD preserves the faithful,
but the proud he pays back in full.*

[24] **Be strong and take heart,
all you who hope in the LORD.**

Thanks for all your prayers…keep them coming!

From My Life to Yours

~ What have you been re-learning on your way to recovery? Are you re-learning physical things like how to walk and talk, or emotional things like how to be happy and love or trust again? I encourage you to make a list and then spend some time praying for God to help you learn what you need to learn in His time and in the mean time, take refuge in Him.

September 6, 2009: Dad Called Me Today

Dad called me on the phone today (well I think Auburn helped, but he did the talking!). I don't remember the exact conversation, but it was the first time I talked to him on the phone since before his assault. He said, "I love you" several times.

I love you too Dad!

September 07, 2009: A Different Type of Grief

To outsiders, it may seem like "all is well" and that we're "doing great" now that Dad is out of the coma and making progress every day. And in some aspects we are doing great. God is sustaining us and we are rejoicing in the progress we do see.

However, there is a different type of grief that we feel.

Losses that we face each day as we learn to deal with the long term effects of Dad's brain injury. It's hard to put into words, but I felt this grief wash over me again last night as I started reading Bob and Lee Woodruff's book, *"In an Instant"* that tells the story of Bob's brain injury and his recovery. As they described the early days and the trauma of it all, I felt a fresh grief fall on me.

Things will never be the same.

And most people won't understand what our family is going through. The shock and the trauma of Dad's assault and injury are beginning to wear off and people are less interested in the day to day happenings. There are a few family and close friends that will walk the entire journey with us, but most won't. And from what I understand, that's pretty normal.

And God is teaching me through all of this.

The lie that I often believe is that people don't care or that people will let me down or disappoint me.

As I was journaling today about some wounds of the past, God reminded me of this truth, *"Shelley, people and institutions are imperfect and will let you down or disappoint you at some point. But,* **_I will never fail you_**. *Put your trust and hope in me. Don't build your life on the foundation of people or institutions but build it* **_in me_**. *Then, when the storms of life come, your 'house' or your life, will stand and survive. Putting your hope and trust in anything else is like building on the sand. When the storms come, your house will be destroyed."*

Wow...so hard to hear. The easy thing for me to do is to depend on people – just like the easy thing to do is to build a house on the sand. It takes more money, more time and more sweat to dig a foundation and mix and pour the cement to have a solid foundation. But, when the storms come (and they will come – John 16:33, *"in this world **you will have trouble**"*) I will be thankful I took the time to build on solid rock. I can get by for a while with the foundation of sand, but not forever. Eventually a trial or "storm" will come that will shake me to the core. And then devastation comes.

And as I wrote in my journal, I felt God asking me this question, *"Which foundation will you choose, Shelley?"*

It will take time, effort and some sweat, but I want to choose the solid rock foundation of Christ. I want to survive the trials and storms that come into my life.

And so, I began looking up scriptures to affirm what God was teaching me. Here's what I found…

Truth #1: Though People Let Me Down, God Will Not Forsake Me

Isaiah 49:14-16
*But Zion said, "The LORD has forsaken me, the Lord has forgotten me." "Can a mother forget the baby at her breast and have no compassion on the child she has borne? **Though she may forget, I will not forget you!** See, I have engraved you on the palms of my hands; your walls are ever before me.*

Psalm 27:10
*Though my father and mother forsake me, **the LORD will receive me**.*

Psalm 94:14
*For **the LORD will not reject his people**; he will never forsake his inheritance.*

Deuteronomy 31:6
*Be strong and courageous. Do not be afraid or terrified because of them, for the LORD your God goes with you; **he will never leave you nor forsake you**.*

Deuteronomy 31:8
*The LORD himself goes before you and will be with you; **he will never leave you nor forsake you**. Do not be afraid; do not be discouraged.*

Joshua 1:5
*No one will be able to stand up against you all the days of your life. As I was with Moses, so I will be with you; **I will never leave you nor forsake you**.*

Psalm 9:10
*Those who know your name will trust in you, **for you, LORD, have never forsaken those who seek you**.*

Hebrews 13:5
*Keep your lives free from the love of money and be content with what you have, because God has said, **"Never will I leave you; never will I forsake you."***

<u>Truth #2</u>: Though People Fail Me, God Will Never Fail Me
Psalm 73:26
My flesh and my heart may fail, but God is the strength of my heart and my portion forever.

Isaiah 51:6
Lift up your eyes to the heavens, look at the earth beneath; the heavens will vanish like smoke, the earth will wear out like a garment and its inhabitants die like flies. ***But my salvation will last forever, my righteousness*** <u>***will never fail***</u>***.***

Lamentations 3:22
Because of the LORD's great love we are not consumed, ***for his compassions*** <u>***never fail***</u>***.***

Corinthians 13:8
Love <u>***never fails***</u>*. But where there are prophecies, they will cease; where there are tongues, they will be stilled; where there is knowledge, it will pass away.*

Acts 5:38
Therefore, in the present case I advise you: Leave these men alone! Let them go! ***For if their purpose or activity is of human origin, it will fail.***

<u>Truth #3</u>: A Foundation in Christ Will Stand Firm Through the Trials of Life

Matthew 7:24-27
"Therefore everyone who hears these words of mine and puts them into practice is like a wise man who built his house on the rock. The rain came down, the streams rose, and the winds blew and beat against that house; ***yet it did not fall, because it had its foundation on the rock****. But everyone who hears these words of mine and does not put them into practice is like a foolish man who built his house on sand. The rain came down, the streams rose, and the winds blew and beat against that house, and it fell with a great crash."*

Luke 6:47-49
I will show you what he is like who comes to me and hears my words and puts them into practice. ***He is like a man building a house, who dug down deep and laid the*** <u>***foundation on rock***</u>***. When a flood came, the torrent struck that house but could not shake it, because it was*** <u>***well built***</u>***.*** *But the one who hears my words and does not put them into practice is like a man who built a house on the ground without a foundation. The moment the torrent struck that house, it collapsed and its destruction was complete."*

2 Timothy 2:19
Nevertheless, ***God's solid foundation*** <u>***stands firm***</u>*, sealed with this inscription: "The Lord knows those who are his," and, "Everyone who confesses the name of the Lord must turn away from wickedness."*

Isaiah 28:16
So this is what the Sovereign LORD says: "See, I lay a stone in Zion, a tested stone, ***a precious cornerstone for a*** <u>***sure foundation***</u>***;*** *the one who trusts will never be dismayed.*

Isaiah 33:5-6
The LORD is exalted, for he dwells on high; he will fill Zion with justice and righteousness. ***He will be the*** <u>***sure foundation***</u> ***for your times,*** *a rich store of salvation and wisdom and knowledge; the fear of the LORD is the key to this treasure.*

1 Corinthians 3:10-15
By the grace God has given me, I laid a foundation as an expert builder, and someone else is building on it. But

each one should be careful how he builds. ***For no one can lay any foundation other than the one already laid, which is Jesus Christ.*** *If any man builds on this foundation using gold, silver, costly stones, wood, hay or straw, his work will be shown for what it is, because the Day will bring it to light. It will be revealed with fire, and the fire will test the quality of each man's work. If what he has built survives, he will receive his reward. If it is burned up, he will suffer loss; he himself will be saved, but only as one escaping through the flames.*

Ephesians 2:19-22
Consequently, you are no longer foreigners and aliens, but fellow citizens with God's people and members of God's household, ***built on the foundation of the apostles and prophets, with Christ Jesus himself as the chief cornerstone.*** *In him the whole building is joined together and rises to become a holy temple in the Lord*

The Moral of the Story?

Until I reach heaven, the storms will continue to come. Pain. Devastation. Heartache. Grief. But, I have the promise that God will walk with me through every single storm. He will never fail me, He will never leave me or forsake me and when my life is built upon His foundation, I <u>will</u> survive whatever comes my way.

From My Life to Yours

~ Which foundation are you choosing? During difficult times it can be tempting to neglect our foundation, and that's the time that it's really tested. Right now I encourage you to stabilize your foundation. Take some time out of your day to spend with God, reading His Word.

September 10, 2009: In An Instant by Bob and Lee Woodruff

Ever since Dad suffered his brain injury, I keep hearing the name Bob Woodruff. In fact, an article in Parade Magazine, *"Can Brains Be Saved,"* came out just days after Dad first entered the hospital. You can read it at the following link: http://www.parade.com/health/2009/07/12-lee-woodruff-can-brains-be-saved.html

Therefore, I decided to read the book, *"In an Instant,"* by Bob and Lee Woodruff about Bob's brain injury and recovery.

Here are a few quotes from the book that I found encouraging,

> *"Each brain injury is highly individual and recovery still remains somewhat of a mystery to medical science. But the more faculties a person has going into an injury – intelligence, motivation, engagement in life, even support from family and friends – the better the prospects for recovery."* [5]

> *"'Think of it this way,' Dr. Armonda said later, 'If you are a person like Bob Woodruff, who is forty-*

four and has made great use of his brain in his life, speaks multiple languages, has an intellectual curiosity and abundant life experiences, you have a better shot at how well those neurons are going to reconnect. Think of those neurons as a road – I-95, for example. If the only way your brain knows how to get from NY to Washington is along I-95, and a giant jackknifed truck closes all lanes of the highway you are in trouble.

But, if you are Bob Woodruff and you know alternate routes, you can take back roads or board Amtrak or hop on the shuttle flight at Regan National.

If you are a person who can come up with other solutions, who has really used your brainpower, you have more chance to develop alternate pathways for cognitive function and reasoning and putting all those neurons together.'

It seemed like a small thing to hang on to – Bob's brilliance – but the analogy gave me comfort. If ever there was a brain that knew how to navigate and use neurons, I thought it was my husband's. Perhaps brainpower and sheer will to live would drive his recovery. With Bob, I knew, anything was possible." [6]

My dad is also a very brilliant man. He's a man with a PhD who runs organizations. A man whom God has greatly gifted and has used in many ways. Therefore, the analogy given above also gave me comfort.

However, Dad also has the benefit of the power of God through prayer! No matter what "road blocks" he may face ahead, we know that God is bigger and able to bring healing to him.

Right now, his brain is trying to find those "alternate routes." Sometimes he gets stuck and can't find his way through. Other times he finds his way through.

We continue to pray that God allows Dad's brain to find those connections and pathways again and that Dad would not give up and that he will continue to persevere.

Marathon, Not a Sprint

They also say in the book that, *"this kind of injury...is complicated. It takes a long time for the brain to heal; it's about patience. Always remember that this is a marathon, not a sprint. Healing from brain injuries can easily take up to 18 months, even 2 years."* [7]

I like the analogy of a marathon vs. a sprint. Especially with CJ being a long distance runner, it makes sense to me. It will take time. Dad is making progress and will continue to do so. We thank everyone for cheering him (and us) on as we run this marathon together.

From My Life to Yours

~ Have you been viewing your road to recovery as a marathon or a sprint? Do you need to re-evaluate your expectations? Take some time right now to write out what your expectations are, and then entrust God with them.

September 10, 2009: Swallowing Test Results

Dad had his swallowing test today and has now officially started on thickened puree food. He will have a pureed lunch tomorrow...yeah!! They will not give him any thin liquids yet.

I'm going to drive over tomorrow for a quick "over and back" one day visit since I work this weekend. See you soon Dad!

September 11, 2009: Eating for the First Time!

Yes, it's true! Dad ate his first meal since his assault July 1st. His lunch consisted of pureed chicken, mashed potatoes, pureed squash, pudding, thickened milk and thickened juice...and he ate it all! He seems thrilled to be eating again (pureed and thickened as it was) and will start getting three meal trays a day! Yeah!

Dad's First Meal!

Spending the Day With Dad and Auburn

I enjoyed entering the world of Dad and Auburn for the day. Dad walked, walked and walked some more (see videos below). During the walks, we sat down to take a breather. Notice Dad's shirt below that one of his friends got for him saying, "A'll Be Bach." Just say it in a low Arnold Schwarzenegger voice and then you'll get it!

Having Fun With Dad!

I enjoyed my visit today. On the way back upstairs from speech therapy Dad decided to walk and so I pushed his wheelchair. As we were getting off the elevator onto his floor Dad was saying something about the wheelchair. And I thought maybe he wanted me to sit in it. So, I sat in the wheelchair and then he wheeled me back to his room!

It actually was fun and I felt like a kid again and said something like, "Woo Hoo!" We took some hairpin turns and barely missed banging my knees a few times. As the nurses looked over at us they yelled out, "Be Careful!" Dad, Auburn and I started laughing and laughed all the way back to the room. Dad did pass his maneuverability skills test, but just barely!

Dad's First Post on the Blog

Auburn and Dad sat down with the laptop today, looked at Yahoo Sports, and Dad dictated his first post to the blog.

Walking, Walking, and More Walking

Dad has improved so much in his walking since I last saw him two weeks ago. Wow! He only requires minimal assistance for guiding and balance. Otherwise, he now holds his own weight!

America the Beautiful

In honor of 9/11, Auburn and Dad sang "America the Beautiful" together. Dad was able to remember most of the words although his singing voice is not quite the same!

From My Life to Yours

~ While Dad's road to recovery is mainly physical, I'm reminded of Jesus' words in Matthew 4, *Man does not live on bread alone, but on every word that comes from the mouth of God.'* (verse 4). None of this would be possible without God, and so today I encourage you to spend time thanking God for what He is doing in your life – whether it's small or large.

September 18, 2009: Preparing to Go Home

Dad will have a "pass" to go home on a visit Sunday. This will be his first time to leave the hospital or nursing home! I don't know if he'll want to go back. He also has a possible discharge date from the hospital this Thursday (9/24/09) just three months since his assault on July 1st. We are asking for prayers for all the discharge planning and preparations!

Stacey will be there this week to help Auburn and Dad prepare for his homecoming.

September 18, 2009: Miracle of the Moment

I don't know about you, but for me, it's so easy to get caught up in planning for the future. By nature, I am a planner. Therefore, this devotion yesterday from "Jesus Calling" by Sarah Young really impacted me. It is written from God's perspective.

"You will not find my peace by engaging in excessive planning: attempting to control what will happen to you in the future. That is a commonly practiced form of unbelief. When your mind spins with multiple plans, peace may sometimes seem to be within your grasp, yet it always eludes you. Just when you think you have prepared for all possibilities, something unexpected pops up and throws things into confusion.

I did not design the human mind to figure out the future. That is beyond your capability. ***I crafted your mind for*** *continual communication with Me. Bring all your needs, your hopes and fears. Commit everything into my care. Turn from the path of planning to the path of peace."*[8]

I was sharing this devotion with my sister, Stacey, and some of the things I am currently dealing with and she mentioned a song by Stephen Curtis Chapman called the "Miracle of the Moment." I've heard this song over and over on the radio and yet never really paid attention to the words. As we're dealing with Dad's transition to home and his next phase of therapy, it's easy to get caught up in planning. And yet, I sense God drawing me back to the present moment with Him. I'm realizing that my most important "task" is to stay in constant communication with God instead of constant activity.

How would my life be different if I stayed in constant communication with God?

I'm not 100% sure, but I do think I would be more peaceful and less worried. Instead of scurrying around in constant action, motion and production, my activity would be birthed out of my relationship with Jesus and listening to Him. Instead of spinning my wheels, I would be listening to God. Then, I would do the most important tasks as He leads me, making my day so much more effective. That's what I want! Lord, empower me by your Spirit to change!

And in the meantime, I want to remember to enjoy the "Miracle of the Moment"....

Lyrics to the Song, Miracle of the Moment by Steven Curtis Chapman:

It's time for letting go

All of our "if onlies"
Cause we don't have a time machine
And even if we did
Would we really want to use it
Would we really want to go change everything
Cause we are who and where and what we are for now
And this is the only moment we can do anything about
So breathe it in and breathe it out
And listen to your heartbeat
There's a wonder in the here and now
It's right there in front of you
And I don't want you to miss the miracle of the moment
There's only One who knows
What's really out there waiting
And all the moments yet to be
And all we need to know
Is He's out there waiting
To Him the future's history
And He has given us a treasure called right now
And this is the only moment we can do anything about
So breathe it in and breathe it out
And listen to your heartbeat
There's a wonder in the here and now
It's right there in front of you
And I don't want you to miss the miracle of the moment
And if it brings you tears
Then taste them as they fall
Let them soften your heart
And if it brings you laughter
Then throw your head back
And let it go
Let it go, yeah
You gotta let it go
And listen to your heartbeat
And breathe it in and breathe it out
And listen to your heartbeat

There's a wonder in the here and now
It's right there in front of you
And I don't want you to miss the miracle of the moment
And breathe it in and breathe it out
And listen to your heartbeat
There's a wonder in the here and now
It's right there in front of you
And I don't want you to miss the miracle of the moment.[9]

From My Life to Yours

~ Are you getting caught up in future planning? I encourage you to pick up your Bible and read through Matthew 6:25-34. Then, write down whatever you feel God is telling you through those passages.

Part Six

A New Beginning

September 21, 2009: Changing of the Seasons

As I was driving yesterday on my spontaneous trip to see family, I was noting all the beautiful leaves changing colors... the changing of the seasons! As I was enjoying the drive, I sensed God saying that just as the seasons are changing and we are entering a new season of fall, we are also entering a new season with Dad... HOME!!

Home with assistance and intensive speech therapy.

This next "season" won't last forever and will bring with it joys and frustrations of its own. However, we are very happy to see the acute, hospital, trach and feeding tube days behind us! Thank you God for the changing of the seasons!

Welcome Home Dinner

Yesterday, Dad and Auburn's neighbors made a welcome home dinner for Dad. He had a home visit scheduled and they wanted to help him celebrate. He should be officially discharged from the hospital sometime this week (possibly Thursday)!

We had a great time and enjoyed yummy pot roast, homemade applesauce and blueberry cobbler. Dad had his food blended up, but ate every bite! He even said the prayer of blessing for our dinner together...already taking leadership of the family again.

My four year old niece, Lauren, seems to be perceptive even in her young age and probably understands more than what we even realize. It was so precious. She kept going over to Dad and giving him hugs, sitting on his lap and wanting him to read her a book. Dad soaked in her love... I'm sure there is a healing property to a grandchild's love. Allie also gave him hugs and enjoyed seeing Grandpa Chuck!

Dad's First View of "Home"

Dad had a quick visit on Saturday to his home. He was so excited! At one point he said it was a "dream" to be back in his home again! This Wednesday it will be 12 weeks! Hard to believe! He was in a coma almost 6 weeks and God has brought him sooooo far the past 6 weeks!

Yesterday, he put on one of his suits and was able to tie his own tie, perfectly! He never ceases to amaze me!

The Greater Impact

Auburn mentioned that yesterday they went to *"the tiny Alpha and Omega church on the corner (down the street from the Akron apartment building). Pastor Angelina Davis saw us and rushed down the aisle weeping, encircled us both in a mighty hug and thanked God.*

*We have been friends for several years and in recent times Chuck had offered her some help and advice about how to sustain and grow her little church. Chuck said, "Hallelujah!" several times along with the praying, weeping women...**Chuck also said, "Many many people will know Him because of what we're doing. People we don't even know about."***

When Auburn told me this story yesterday, I had tears in my eyes - tears of joy. It will not only be amazing to see

Dad's full recovery but to continue to see the good God brings out of this tragedy.

Visit in Cambridge, Ohio

Stacey is in Barberton this week helping prepare the house for Dad's homecoming. Her girls spent the weekend with Grandma and Grandpa Reeder so yesterday she went to Cambridge, Ohio to pick them up and have lunch with Mom and Chet.

I hadn't planned on being in Akron/Barberton this past weekend, but at the last minute, I felt a prompting to drive over for the occasion! I'm not usually a spontaneous person, but at 10am decided to go and by 10:30am I was in the car on my way. I went to Cambridge and spent some time with Mom, Chet, Stacey, Lauren and Allie. It had been only three weeks since I last saw my nieces, but we've spent so much time together lately that it felt like longer. It made my day when both Lauren and Allie came running to me, giving me BIG hugs!! There's nothing like the love of a child to make it all worthwhile!

After our visit, we headed up to Barberton for Dad's welcome home dinner.

I was home by 9:30pm and know that I'll never regret taking the time to be with family and make these memories. We have learned to treasure each moment we have together!

From My Life to Yours

~ When was the last time you celebrated something? If you can't think of anything to celebrate, read through your list of "ups". You can celebrate by getting together with friends and family, or just taking the time to do something for yourself (like taking a bubble bath or buying yourself a new shirt). Remember that Jesus came that we might have life to the full (John 10:10).

September 26, 2009: Visiting Dad at Home

CJ and I went to Barberton Thursday night expecting a short 15-30 minute visit with Dad. However, each time we got up to leave, he insisted we stay longer. So, we ended up having a great 2-hour visit with him!

He is now home and is looking great. There was a night-and-day difference from my visit with him on Sunday, just four days earlier. He seemed so much more alert and had a brightness in his eyes that shined through! I think we'd all agree that there's just no place like home.

This was the first time I've seen him in regular clothes for a while and he looked so normal...polo shirt, khakis, belt, dress shoes... And the great thing is that he is on absolutely NO medications and is now eating regular food.

Great Conversation

We had some great conversation...some of the best I've had w/ him. At one point I asked him if he still feels like he comes in and out of a "fog" and he said no. He said he is now in a go— fog. I didn't completely understand him and asked him if he was in a good fog. He said, "No! I am in a God fog."

I thought about it for a moment and decided that's where I want to be as well! A God fog. Surrounded by His presence and walking in His Spirit. Earlier that day, I had read the following verse that talks about walking in the presence of the Lord, or in a "God fog!"

"Blessed are those who...walk in the light of your presence, O LORD." Psalm 89:15

I also mentioned to Dad that I believed God is going to use him as an inspiration to many and already is. Dad said, "Yes! I would like that!"

I don't remember all the details of our conversation, but felt encouraged after we left. My dad is improving. And we are all learning to live in a "God fog." God is so good!

I Saw God Today

As we were traveling to Virginia this weekend, CJ played the song, "I Saw God Today" by George Strait. As I listened to it, tears streamed down my face. I felt an overwhelming sense that "I saw God today" as I have witnessed God working miracles in my Dad's recovery everyday. And miracles in my heart.

Lyrics to the song, I Saw God Today by George Strait:

I just walked down the street to the coffee shop

had to take a break
I'd been by her side for eighteen hours straight
I saw a flower growing in the middle of the sidewalk
pushing up through the concrete
like it was planted right there for me to see
the flashin' lights, the honkin' horns
all seemed to fade away
in the shadow of that hospital at 5:08
I saw God today

Chorus:
I've been to church
I've read the book
I know He's here, but I don't look
near as often as I should
Yeah, I know I should
His fingerprints are everywhere
I'd just slow down to stop and stare
opened my eyes and man I swear
I saw God today

I saw a couple walking by they were holding hands
Man, she had that glow
yeah I couldn't help but notice she was starting to show
I stood there for a minute takin' in the sky
lost in that sunset
a splash of amber melted in the shades of red
Chorus
I got my face pressed up against the nursery glass
She's sleeping like a rock
My name on her wrist wearing tiny pink socks
She's got my nose, she's got her mama's eyes
My brand new baby girl
She's a miracle

I saw God today[10]

October 8, 2009: Dad's New Smile

Well, today was the big day! After seeing the dentist, Dad came home with two new front teeth! After 14 weeks of enduring a toothless grin, he now is all smiles. What a blessing - and what a morale booster for Dad.

I literally shouted for joy when I received the picture on my phone of Dad with his new front teeth and his new smile. I called and talked to him on the phone and he said he looked pretty.

This was the last outward "visible" sign of his assault on July 1, 2009. And although he still has a long road ahead of him with his speech therapy and cognitive therapy, he is looking more and more like himself everyday. We have so much to be thankful for.

From My Life to Yours

~ Take some time right now to think and pray on the question: How can you see God in your life right now? Write it down.

October 11, 2009: Dad's Visit to Findlay

Dad and Auburn made their first visit back to Findlay since July! They came over to MawMaw and PawPaw's for a visit on Sunday for some of MawMaw's famous Pumpkin Pie! Dad ate two pieces...yummy!

PawPaw played his harmonica for us and Dad joined in singing with him! How touching! PawPaw hasn't played his harmonica since his stroke last year but recently picked it up again this past week. So, to see PawPaw who is recovering from brain damage from a stroke and Dad who is recovering from brain damage from a TBI singing and playing together was truly a God-moment!

We also had a great visit with Homer Lentz. It was filled with positive memories, healing moments and God's love evident through Homer. What a blessing to have friends like him praying and supporting our family. We love you Homer!

It was also great to have Dad and Auburn visit us at our house Saturday evening! What a blessing to have my dad sitting in the recliner in my living room. We had a great talk about some of the emotional healing that has been taking place within Dad (Auburn will post more on this later). I truly believe that God is still at work within my dad bringing healing to him physically, emotionally and spiritually. And I am seeing it firsthand! As I Corinthians 2:9 says, *"No eye has seen, no ear has heard, no mind has conceived what God has prepared for those who love him."*

From My Life to Yours

~ Can you think of any "God-moments" that you have experienced lately? If so, write them down on your list of "ups". If not, I encourage you to watch for them in the days that come.

October 18, 2009: A Week of Ups and Downs; A Week of Healing

This week has been rough on me emotionally and spiritually for various reasons. It seemed as if my emotions would go up and down to each extreme and then stay mostly down. And I don't think that the weather helped… it has suddenly gotten much more dreary and cold in Ohio!

God's Been Working to Bring Healing to My Heart

God has really been working in my heart regarding some hurt, bitterness and unforgiveness I've held in my heart over some things that happened in a church split years ago. It's been hard to face it, but I know it is necessary. I actually thought I had already dealt with it. So, it was humbling when I sensed God convicting me recently that I still had stuff to surrender to Him.

As the saying goes, *"Bitterness is like taking poison and expecting the other person to die from it."* It really only eats away at me. And so, I've been on a journey of forgiveness and healing this week.

God's Been Working to Bring Healing to Dad's Heart

As I was going through this time of healing, my dad was also going on a healing journey of his own. He called me Tuesday crying. He told me over and over, *"I'm sorry. I'm so sorry."* It was difficult to understand everything he said but Auburn later told me that *"He said he wants to make amends to everybody. He wants his sins wiped away."* Wow. As we have been praying for Dad's physical healing we have also been praying for his emotional and spiritual healing as well. And we are seeing it happen. As Auburn said on her blog this past Wednesday, *"We're in a season of recommitment to our faith, learning where life and hope live for us, and letting spiritual shifts occur on deeper levels. It's becoming more clear to us where to let go and where to cling."*

Praise God for the healing that continues to be evident…I give God all the credit for what we continue to witness in my dad's life. Please continue to pray for Dad (and Auburn's) spiritual, emotional and physical health. Your prayers are powerful!

Here is a note from an e-mail update David Coolidge sent out to Church of God Ministers this week about Dad. It is a note from one of my dad's friends, Tim Schrock.

Dear David,

I was at Gulf Coast Bible College with Chuck Sandstrom in 1970. He ended up graduating from Warner Southern. He also has a doctoral degree.

Last night I had a tremendous blessing. I talked with Chuck Sandstrom on the phone. Though it was hard to make out many of his words, the energy in his voice excited me. His wife, Auburn, says he really comes alive when his friends call him. If you have not been to his blog recently, please do so: chuckscircleoflove.blogspot.com. Chuck told me repeatedly that he is giving his life anew to God. I believe God is going to use Chuck in ways he has not been used before. If you would be so inclined to call Chuck, you both will be blessed.

In His Grip,
Tim Schrock

A "Complete Healing"

I am very saddened today as I found out that a close family friend of ours, Beth Rarey, passed away two days ago. Over the last year, she has had a battle with a brain tumor. Her children wrote on their blog, *"Mom went to be with Jesus today at 3:45 pm. We knew this morning that she was very close so she was surrounded by friends and family. She was very peaceful and had no pain. We will update funeral arrangements as soon as possible.* **We know that now she is completely healed** *and walking the streets of gold!"* (http://www.blogginforthenoggin.com/)

I have been inspired by Beth's daughters, Lindsay and Emily, and their faith in God. About a month ago Lindsay shared some of her thoughts about faith in her blog at: http://peanuttrail.blogspot.com/2009/09/what-if.html.

I am sad and grieving for their family. But, I am also rejoicing that Beth is with Jesus. No more pain. No more tears. Eternal life and unconditional love. Wow.

So a week of ups and downs. A week of healing.

I have been meditating on Psalm 34 this week and thought it would be a good way to end this blog post.

1 I will extol the LORD at all times;
his praise will always be on my lips.

2 My soul will boast in the LORD;
let the afflicted hear and rejoice.

3 Glorify the LORD with me;
let us exalt his name together.

4 I sought the LORD, and he answered me;
he delivered me from all my fears.

5 Those who look to him are radiant;
their faces are never covered with shame.

6 This poor man called, and the LORD heard him;
he saved him out of all his troubles.

7 The angel of the LORD encamps around those who fear him,
and he delivers them.

8 Taste and see that the LORD is good;
blessed is the man who takes refuge in him.

9 Fear the LORD, you his saints,
for **those who fear him lack nothing.**

10 The lions may grow weak and hungry,
but those who seek the LORD lack no good thing.

11 Come, my children, listen to me;
I will teach you the fear of the LORD.

12 Whoever of you loves life
and desires to see many good days,

13 keep your tongue from evil
and your lips from speaking lies.

14 Turn from evil and do good;
seek peace and pursue it.

15 The eyes of the LORD are on the righteous
and his ears are attentive to their cry;

16 the face of the LORD is against those who do evil,
to cut off the memory of them from the earth.

17 **The righteous cry out, and the LORD hears them;**
he delivers them from <u>all</u> their troubles.

18 **The LORD is close to the brokenhearted**
and saves those who are crushed in spirit.

19 **A righteous man may have many troubles,**
but the LORD delivers him from them <u>all</u>;

20 he protects all his bones,
not one of them will be broken.

*21 Evil will slay the wicked;
the foes of the righteous will be condemned.*

*22 The LORD redeems his servants;
no one will be condemned who takes refuge in him.*

From My Life to Yours

~ Are you holding onto any hurt, bitterness or unforgiveness? If so, I encourage you to write down what you are struggling with and then ask God to help you start down the road of healing and forgiveness.

October 21, 2009: Saying Goodbye to a Family Friend

I went to one of the most beautiful funerals I've ever been to today for Beth Rarey. Wow. What a legacy she left behind and what a life she lived, living out her faith in Jesus. So many people came today to honor and celebrate her life. I cried seeing pictures of her holding her grandchildren, knowing that she won't be able to create more memories with them. And yet, what a comfort to know that she is now in heaven with Jesus.

The funeral was held at Stonebridge Church of God, a church that holds many memories for me. A church where my parents were pastors for many years. And we were able to see so many familiar faces and friends that we haven't seen in years, give hugs and re-connect. In some ways, it felt like a reunion of sorts. And it was healing for me.

They ended the funeral with a powerful song called, "I Can Only Imagine" (by Mercy Me). Wow…I can only imagine…but Beth is no longer imagining. She is there with Jesus!

From My Life to Yours

~ It's never easy to watch someone else go through a tragedy, and even the loss of a life of someone going to heaven is traumatic for those left behind. Right now I just want to encourage you to encourage someone else who is going through a different tragedy than you. Whether through a simple card or even just a hug, let them know that even in the midst of your own tragedy, you still care for them.

October 21, 2009: Dad Will Be Visiting Findlay Again

It is now 16.5 weeks since Dad's initial injury. And he will be venturing to Findlay for the second time. However, this time he will be without Auburn. She will be taking a much needed break to rest and refresh. While she is away, Dad will spend each night with her parents, Jerry and Ann Sheaffer, and then spend the afternoons and dinner time with us.

Stacey and the girls will also be coming into town this weekend. And this is the last weekend MawMaw and PawPaw are in Findlay before they leave for Florida for the winter. So, it will be a weekend filled with family time.

I am looking forward to having this time with Dad, but have to admit it will be different. I'm not sure exactly what we'll do or how much stimulation he will be able to tolerate and how much rest time he'll need. There are many questions running through my mind.

And I have to admit that I feel a bit insecure about caring for my dad. I want to respect him and his independence and yet not put him at risk for falls (since his balance is still improving). I want to communicate with him, but not cause frustration for him when his words won't come out right (since he often deals with aphasia and speech difficulties). I don't want to be bossy and yet I want to make sure he takes smaller bites at meals and swallows completely with each bite of food to decrease his risk for aspiration (since his swallowing muscles are still gaining strength).

And I feel inadequate.

And yet, I know that this life is not up to me. There's this still small voice that says to me, *"Shelley, the battle is not yours, it is God's. It's not up to you to figure it all out."*

And so, I can place all my fears, all my inadequacies, all my questions into the hands of Jesus. I can allow Him to lead and guide me. And I can relax and enjoy this stage of life with my dad...however imperfect we all may be. I can learn to treasure each moment.

"Life isn't about waiting for the storm to pass; it's about learning to dance in the rain."

I want to learn how to dance in the rain.

From My Life to Yours

~ Are you suffering from any feelings of inadequacy? If so, I encourage you to lay them at God's feet and ask Him to help you learn to dance in the rain.

October 23, 2009: The Way of Forgiveness: Living Forgiving

On October 10, 2009, **my dad chose to <u>forgive</u> Michael**, the man who assaulted him. My dad's life has been changed forever through this one moment in time and he continues to heal a little more each day from his traumatic brain injury.

And today, I was faced with my own issues with Michael. They still have not found him and so, to me, there doesn't feel like there is closure yet. And yet, there are emotions I need to deal with. Unforgiveness, bitterness, resentment. And I feel led to share from my journal, the journey God led me on today.

Lord, what about Michael?

> "Let him go. Let him be judged by my courts. Let him face his <u>true</u> punishment. Mine. You will accomplish nothing by ensuring that he is judged severely here on earth. Pray for him. I will not let this go unjudged or unpunished. Either he will take full punishment for his crime against your dad and your family or Jesus will take it for him, just as he will take the punishment for your sins. Let Michael go. It is not your responsibility to judge him or fix him. Leave him in my hands."

Jesus said in Matthew 7:1-5, *"Do not judge, or you too will be judged. For in the same way you judge others, you will be judged, and with the measure you use, it will be measured to you. Why do you look at the speck of sawdust in your brother's eye and pay no attention to the plank in your own eye?*

How can you say to your brother, 'Let me take the speck out of your eye,' when all the time there is a plank in your own eye? You hypocrite, first take the plank out of your own eye, and then you will see clearly to remove the speck from your brother's eye."

"Do not judge, and you will not be judged. Do not condemn, and you will not be condemned. Forgive, and you will be forgiven. Give, and it will be given to you. A good measure, pressed down, shaken together and running over, will be poured into your lap. For with the measure you use, it will be measured to you." (Luke 6:37-38)

Romans 2:1 says, *"You, therefore, have no excuse, you who pass judgment on someone else, for at whatever point you judge the other, you are condemning yourself, because you who pass judgment do the same things."*

Not judging someone doesn't mean I never approach them about the wrong they have done.

Galatians 6:1-2 says, *"Brothers, if someone is caught in a sin, you who are spiritual should restore him gently. But watch yourself, or you also may be tempted. Carry each other's burdens, and in this way you will fulfill the law of Christ."*

It means I make sure I look at myself first and have God search my heart for my own sin, the "plank" in my eye so to speak. David said in Psalm 51:3, *"For I know my transgressions and my sin is always before me."* And I know I am guilty of judging Michael.

> "Shelley, I don't want you to sit in the judgment seat of Michael, let Me. I will take care of this. I want your heart to be filled with My love.
>
> Not anger, bitterness or resentment. Allow my Spirit, my light to drive out the darkness in your heart. I have called you out of the darkness and into my marvelous light. (I Peter 2:9) Let me take care of it. Trust me. Release your control of it.
>
> For as Matthew 18:21-35 clearly says – unforgiveness places you in a prison where you will be tortured. I have set you free, forgiven you and rescued you from darkness. Don't allow this to imprison you again. Let it go. Let it go. Leave Michael to me. And trust me with what happens.

> Keep your eyes and your focus on Me and on your own sin. Don't get so focused on everyone else's sin. You have enough to handle of your own. It is not your responsibility to make sure justice is served. It is Mine. And whoever welcomes one of my children, welcomes Me. Whoever messes with one of my children, messes with Me."

"Things that cause people to sin are bound to come, but woe to that person through whom they come. It would be better for him to be thrown into the sea with a millstone tied around his neck than for him to cause one of these little ones to sin. So watch yourselves." Luke 17:1-2

> I do not take this lightly, Shelley. I will take care of Michael. Leave him to Me.

"If your brother sins, rebuke him, and if he repents, forgive him. If he sins against you seven times in a day, and seven times comes back to you and says, 'I repent,' forgive him." Luke 17:3-4

> Shelley, my way is a way of forgiveness. It is one of the central themes of My life and ministry. As I said on the cross, *"Father forgive them for they know not what they are doing."* (Luke 23:34) I ask you to forgive Michael, for he knows not what he has done and the depth of the pain he has caused you and your family.

"And whenever you stand praying, if you have anything against anyone, forgive him and let it drop (leave it, let it go), in order that your Father Who is in heaven may also forgive you your [own] failings and shortcomings and let them drop." Mark 11:25 (AMP)

Lord, today I choose to forgive Michael. I let go of my anger, bitterness and resentment of him – for what he has done to my dad and our family. I leave it in your hands and let it drop from mine. I trust that you will take care of this and I allow you to be the ultimate judge no matter what the earthly courts decide. I will never agree that what Michael did was right but I release him and his crime to you today. I choose the way of forgiveness and ask you to empower me to live forgiving in my actions and words towards Michael. Empower me to love my enemies and pray for those who persecute me (Matthew 5:44). Empower me to overcome evil with good (Romans 12:21).

"Do not take revenge, my friends, but leave room for God's wrath, for it is written: 'It is mine to avenge; I will repay,' says the Lord. On the contrary: 'If your enemy is hungry, feed him; if he is thirsty, give him something to drink. In doing this, you will heap burning coals on his head." Romans 12:19-20

Empower me Lord to live the life You have called me to live. I pray that you would take care of Michael…his judgment, his crime and his soul.

I pray you would be working in his life and his heart to bring him to You. This would truly be a miracle, Lord.

"Do not repay evil with evil or insult with insult, but with blessing, because to this you were called so that you may inherit a blessing." 1 Peter 3:9

Thank you Lord for what you are doing in my heart, setting me free from this unforgiveness, bitterness and resentment. Thank you for empowering me through Your Holy Spirit to walk this out every day, even when I don't feel like it.

I praise You Lord for all the miracles we are seeing in Dad's life and the physical, emotional and spiritual healing you are bringing to him.

"You (Michael) intended to harm me, but God intended it for good, to accomplish what is now being done, the saving of many lives." (Genesis 50:20).

From My Life to Yours

~ Are you ready to take the step of forgiving those who harmed you? No matter what your answer is, I encourage you to pray and ask God to help you in this area. No matter what, it isn't easy, but with God all things are possible.

October 25, 2009: Ohio State Football at MawMaw and PawPaw's

Yesterday Dad and Auburn joined us for some good ole' Buckeye football. Dad was loudly cheering on the team each time they made a touchdown and enjoyed some coffee and cookies with us. It went much better than I anticipated. Dad seemed to tolerate the activity and stimulation well and the girls did pretty good at playing quietly. They found a great little spot for a "clubhouse" behind one of MawMaw's recliners and played for a long time back there.

Auburn updated us on all the activities and therapy we should be helping Dad with during his stay in Findlay. She will be going home to hopefully get some much needed rest, although she did end up planning some meetings during this time as well.

Dad will be with us the next four days from around 2pm until bedtime. I will be giving him some P.T. and the girls will color with him as well as other activities. We may even see have him try the Wii with MawMaw and PawPaw!

October 27, 2009: YMCA Works and the Posture Nazi

Yesterday Dad got a good workout with CJ at the YMCA. He pedaled on the arm bike for ½ mile and then rode the recumbent bike for 1 mile. CJ also had him on the back extension machine, the leg extension machine and the leg press.

Afterwards Dad said he was tired and got a good workout! CJ is definitely a tough "coach." And he worked out at the YMCA with CJ again today…way to go Dad!

Yesterday we also worked on his PVC pegboard that his therapist wants him to work on everyday. He has a diagram to follow and then puts the pieces together according to the diagram. Reminds me of a plumbing job he might have to do on one of his rentals! But, he wasn't really into it. He did two and then hung his head in his hands. Auburn had told me he didn't really like this activity but the therapist thought it was important. So I asked him if he was bored. He said it was boring. Later he called it a "dumb thing." It probably is draining for him mentally and I wouldn't blame him for calling it boring.

We also did some P.T. work with his posture and stretching. Auburn had asked me if I would do some stretching work with him and boy is he tight in his neck, shoulders and back! But, if you think about it, he has been primarily lying in bed or sitting for most of the day the last 17 weeks.

I had him sit on the edge of his chair and gave him tactile cues to sit up straight. I then gave him feedback in a mirror for how he looked sitting straight and then sitting slouched and asked him which he liked better. He said the one sitting up straight! I would have him watch the clock and hold it for 30 seconds. You wouldn't think that would be too hard, but it wore him out using muscles that are weak and stretching muscles that have gotten tight. I told him at dinner that I tell my patients in the clinic that I am the "posture Nazi" and he said really loud "POSTURE NAZI!" and laughed.

We had a good meal of salmon, green beans and rolls and then Stacey dropped him back off at the Sheaffer's for the night. He watched Jeopardy and Glenn Beck with him before he called it a night!

During the last few days, I've noticed that Dad's speech is not as good as I thought it was. He is really still having a lot of difficulty speaking. He will start out with a thought and be unable to finish it. He is able to say short sentences well and seems to perk up and do better for short telephone conversations or visitors.

I was talking to someone today about this and realized that he is still not very far along in his recovery. Many doctors say to give him 1-2 years for full recovery and that the brain can continue to make modification and adaptations even after that time period.

But, if you think about 2 years being ~100 weeks and that he is now 17 weeks after his initial injury, then he really is only about 17% of his total recovery time. And he is doing so well, so soon. Even the doctors have commented on that. Everyone keeps saying "It takes time. It takes time." And, so I have to trust that God is continuing His healing work within my dad and that he will in time continue to improve.

We appreciate continued prayers for Dad's physical, emotional and spiritual healing.

From My Life to Yours

~ Even as life starts to return to normal – well, more normal anyway – it's important to remember that the journey will continue. I come back to this being a marathon, not a sprint. So right now I encourage you to pray for patience in the days to come.

October 27, 2009: Visits from Friends and Playing the Wii

Tonight Dad had two visitors. One was David Clark, former Findlay Chief of Police and Pastor here in the local area. They had a great visit!

He was also visited by Ben Mitchell, a good friend. Ben told me, "I wouldn't be who I am today if it wasn't for your dad." Ben and Dad ministered together at Stonebridge Church of God for years.

Dad did better talking tonight and seems to do better when he has visitors. He comes alive and engages with people with the same charisma he's always had!

Playing Wii at MawMaw and PawPaw's

MawMaw fixed us dinner again tonight (thank you MawMaw!) and afterwards we played a game of bowling on the Wii. Dad actually did much better than I thought he would do.

He got 2 spares and a strike right away and ended up with 111 points. Way to go Dad!! He seems to always exceed my expectations! He was laughing, cheering and clapping for each spare and strike throughout the game.

Stacey leaves in the morning with the girls. It's been a good visit and we'll miss them.

We'll have one more evening with Dad during his visit to Findlay!

October 27, 2009: God is Providing

Last week, on October 21st, Dad was officially "laid off" from his position as the Executive Director of the Barberton Community Foundation. He told me several times that this was his "dream job" and where he wanted to be until he retired. So it was bittersweet.

But, we were praying about how the Foundation could help Dad in his recovery and I believe God gave us this idea: to ask the Foundation if they would be willing to purchase Dad and Auburn's house in Barberton as an investment in their community.

You see, Dad bought that house specifically for that job at the Barberton Community Foundation. They requested he live in Barberton and so he immediately went out and bought a house. It was brand new when they bought it a year ago and is in a new development. In the last several months, Dad and Auburn have been able to figure out how to manage just about everything except the mortgage of that house.

And so, when they met with the Foundation last week, Dad and Auburn requested that the Foundation consider purchasing it.

And God provided.

The Foundation called the next day saying they would buy the house! We give a BIG thank you to the Foundation for their generous support of my dad during this difficult time and to God for His continued provision.

There are still many unknowns for my dad and Auburn. But, we can see God at work clearing the way for them, guiding them each step of the way. And providing for their every need. In big and small ways.

Thank you for your continued prayers!

"And my God will liberally supply (fill to the full) your every need according to His riches in glory in Christ Jesus." Philippians 4:19 (AMP)

From My Life to Yours

~ We've talked a lot about paying attention to the "ups" on the road to recover, but today I encourage you to focus on all the different kinds of things that God has been providing for you.

October 28, 2009: Yahtzee and Another Good Day

Dad came over for dinner again tonight and afterwards we played a game of Yahtzee. He actually remembered it quite well, got the only Yahtzee of the game and beat us all! Way to go Dad!

After getting good rest, he was much clearer in his speech tonight. He still struggles to find the words, but was able to complete thoughts and have a good dialogue with CJ and I.

CJ worked him out again at the YMCA today. Anyone that knows Dad, knows that he is a hard worker. And he has stepped up to the challenge of working out with CJ this week! I think it's been good for him to get the extra exercise and workouts.

When Stacey, Lauren and Allie were leaving this morning, CJ asked Lauren "What was your favorite part of the weekend?" She simply replied, "Seeing Grandpa Chuck." When we told Dad her response tonight, he had tears in his eyes. The love of a child!

It's been a good day and was a good week visiting with Dad.

I leave tomorrow for a speaking engagement in Wisconsin this weekend. But, Dad's brother, Bill will be coming in to Findlay tomorrow to visit with Dad and will stay with CJ at our house. It will be great for Dad to see his brother!

October 30, 2009: Finding My Pony

I was reminded today of the story below today.

"There were two boys who were the subject of an experiment. One was put into a room with every toy known to children. The other boy was put into a room full of horse manure. They were left alone for quite a while, and then the doctor conducting the experiment came to check on them.

He found the boy who was in the room of toys, sitting on the side, looking dejected. When questioned, he said that the reason he was so upset was that there was no Nintendo DS in the room. That was his favorite toy.

The doctor went to check on the second boy, and to his surprise, found him jumping around, dancing, singing, laughing and having a grand time. When questioned as to how he could possibly be so happy in a room filled with horse manure, he responded, 'With this much horse manure, there MUST be a pony in here somewhere!'"
Author Unknown

As we've been walking through these last few months, it has felt like we've been in a room filled with horse manure. However, instead of looking at my circumstances and feeling overwhelmed with all the "manure," so to speak, in my life, I want to look for my "pony," and the good God is going to bring out of all of this.

Because with all the tragedy and trials we've gone through and continue to walk through, there <u>must</u> be a pony in there somewhere!

From My Life to Yours

~ Can you see a "pony" somewhere in you field of "manure"? While the "ups" are good encouragers, there is also a much bigger picture that we can't always see. Today

I encourage you to pray for God to help you see the bigger picture – to find your pony.

Part Seven

The Hope Continues

December 6, 2009: Dad's Speech He Wrote and Delivered

Here is the transcript of the speech Dad gave at last night's fundraising event. Auburn says, "The greatest moment for most of us last night came when Chuck looked up from the page, leveled his eyes at us all and declared with great power, 'I intend to emerge fully!' A spontaneous ovation erupted."

Here's the speech Dad wrote and delivered....

It's good to see so many friends here.

I want to try to express to you where I am in my journey. I am aware that there was an assault but I do not remember it. I have been in a number of situations in that neighborhood but never felt I had a cause for fear. Neighbors have said the police misjudged the seriousness of the threat to me that night when they failed to arrest the assailant.

We can't go back and make it right so we must find a way to go forward.

I am aware that I have a severe brain injury and that it affects my short-term memory and my communications. It was hard for us to experience the loss of my position and to let go of our home. My wife Auburn carries an overwhelming burden and does it with great love. So often, I am powerless to help, but I am aware of all that is going on around me.

It is frustrating for me to try to express a complete thought and then hear something muddled come out. I understand others perfectly well but I am not always able to make myself understood. If you look in my eyes rather than listen to my words, you will see that I'm here.

In light of all this tragedy and loss, where can we put our focus? We have determined to rely on God and to focus on the things over which we do have some control. It IS possible to build physical strength, flexibility and balance. It IS possible to work diligently on cognitive and speech issues. It IS possible to stay involved in the community.

We have built a grass-roots, out of pocket program, to address the things we can positively affect in my recovery. These first one to two years will be critical in my life-long outcome. It is a choice between attention to details or neglect of details.

Someone will help me re-learn computer keyboarding or they will not. Someone will help me stretch the tendons in my ankles or they will not. Someone will take me golfing or they will not. We've learned that many people in my predicament are simply warehoused or propped up in front of a TV and never have an opportunity to emerge.

I intend to emerge and to emerge fully. I need the commitment of friends and community members to keep me IN the center of LIFE rather than IN the margins. I need opportunities to re-access, practice and regain dozens of skills, large and small.

Above all, we need the financial support to continue this aggressive physical and cognitive program. We're shooting for an amount to carry us to July of 2010, one full year after the assault.

Auburn has said that if we keep prayer, laughter and affection in the center of our lives, we'll be able to face and accomplish anything. We are inviting you to join us in this story of prayer, laughter, affection and success.

I hope in one to two years to be able to celebrate with you a story of dramatic restoration and new life.

We are so grateful for your faithfulness, help and friendship.

From My Life to Yours

~ You might not be giving a speech to a room full of people any time soon, but I encourage you to reflect on the past and write down what you would say if you had the opportunity.

January 30, 2011: An Update

I wanted to share a brief update.

October 15, 2010:

"Fugitive task force arrests man accused of putting former Barberton foundation director into coma"

By Phil Trexler
Beacon Journal staff writer
A 15-month search for a man accused of severely beating the former director of the Barberton Community Foundation ended Monday....

January 19, 2011:

Michael pleaded guilty to a charge a Felonious Assault a felony of the 2nd degree. The sentencing guideline for this degree of a crime can range at a minimum of 2 yrs. to a maximum of 8 yrs. There is a presumption a defendant will receive a prison commitment on this degree of a crime. Michael was given a 4 yr. prison commitment today.

Read the prosecutor's report at:
http://chuckscircleoflove.blogspot.com/2011/01/11911-from-prosecutors-office.html

January 30, 2011:

Feature article in the Akron Beacon Journal about my dad, Chuck Sandstrom's forgiveness toward Michael.

What's next?

My dad is not giving up. Although he continues with permanent effects from his injury, he wants to work. Therefore, he is launching a new business called, "Chuck Sandstrom Enterprises, Inc" to share his story, motivational presentations, as well as consult with organizations. You can find out more at his website here: www.ChuckSandstrom.org

Thank you for your prayers...

Thank you for your prayers and support through this last year and a half. We have witnessed miracles and continue to see God's hand at work.
Please continue to pray for Michael, his family and his children. Michael has asked for my dad's forgiveness in a letter of apology. "At sentencing, Michael was asked if he had anything to say before he was sentenced. He did say he was sorry for what he had done, and the harm he caused to the Sandstrom's. He told the Judge he wants to take full advantage of the programs offered at the institution to work on his anger/anger management as well as AA meetings to change for the better for when he is released."

Pray that Michael truly changes through the power of Christ.

From My Life to Yours

~ The very first thing I asked you to do when starting this book was to write down the facts – what you knew to be true. While the original facts were correct, I encourage you to reflect on them now – what are the new facts? What has changed or improved during the time that you spent working through this book?

The Story Continues...

Read the continuation of the story at my dad and Auburn's blog: www.chuckscircleoflove.com

Invite my dad, Chuck Sandstrom to speak at your event: www.chucksandstrom.org

Listen to Shelley share a presentation about when bad things happen titled, "Unshackled and Grace-full" here: www.christianspeakers.tv/badthings

Shelley Hitz

Shelley Hitz has been writing and publishing books since 2008. She is also the author of the website, FindYourTrueBeauty.com, that reaches thousands of girls each month around the world. Her openness and vulnerability, as she shares her own story of hope and healing, will inspire and encourage you.

Shelley has been ministering to teens since 1998 alongside her husband, CJ. They currently travel and speak to teens and adults around the country. Shelley's main passion is to share God's truth and the freedom in Christ she has found with others. She does this through her books, websites and speaking engagements. You can find more about Shelley at www.BodyandSoulPublishing.com or invite her to speak at your event here: www.ChristianSpeakers.tv

Shelley's Other Books:

**21 Days of Gratitude Challenge:
Finding Freedom from Self-Pity
and a Negative Attitude**
by Shelley Hitz

**Unshackled and Free:
True Stories of Forgiveness**
by CJ and Shelley Hitz

**The Forgiveness Formula:
Finding Lasting Freedom in Christ**
by CJ and Shelley Hitz

**Mirror Mirror…Am I Beautiful?
Looking Deeper to Find Your True Beauty**
by Shelley Hitz

Teen Devotionals…for Girls!
By Shelley Hitz and Heather Hart

Get Free Christian Books

Get notified of our book promotions and download Shelley's eBook, "How to Find Free Christian Books Online" at:

http://www.bodyandsoulpublishing.com/freebooks

Index of Entries

Introduction 1

July 1, 2009: About My Dad's Assault 5

July 23, 2009: Visiting Pity City 8

July 23, 2009: Breakthrough to Hope 9

July 23, 2009: Dad Squeezed My Hand 11

July 24, 2009: Dad's Next Facility 12

July 25, 2009: Back to the Basics 13

July 26, 2009: Fearing the Future 14

July 26, 2009: Tips for Caregivers 18

July 26, 2009: On the Road Again 20

July 26, 2009: When the Sun Shines 21

July 26, 2009: At the Hospital With Dad 23

July 26, 2009: Praying for Grandpa Chuck 24

July 27, 2009: A Few Highlights from Today 26

July 28, 2009: The Tidal Wave of Emotions 27

July 28, 2009: Dad Stood on His Feet in Therapy Today! 31

July 29, 2009: Faith That Can Move Mountains 35

July 29, 2009: Heart of Gratitude 41

July 30, 2009: The Jesus Prayer from Terry Bohannon 42

July 31, 2009: Great Progress in Therapy 43

July 31, 2009: Speech Therapy 44

August 1, 2009: Lauren's Visit and a Smile 46

August 2, 2009: New Movements 47

August 2, 2009: Rebuilding After a Storm 48

August 3, 2009: Progress and Changes 53

August 4, 2009: Encouragement for Today 58

August 5, 2009: More Movement 60

August 6, 2009: Be Still and Know 63

August 7, 2009: Spending the Day with Dad 64

August 8, 2009: Starting to Get My Dad Back 69

August 10, 2009: Lots of Time with Dad 72

August 11, 2009: Battling Resentment 74

August 11, 2009: Back in Findlay 77

August 12, 2009: Sacrifices Made 79

August 13, 2009: It Feels Like a Miracle 80

August 17, 2009: The Love of a Father 82

August 17, 2009: Visiting Hours Update 84

August 19, 2009: Hearing Dad Talk for the First Time 87

August 20, 2009: Resistance Verses Routine 91

August 21, 2009: Last Day of Therapy at Manor Care 92

August 21, 2009: The Greater Impact Dad is Having 93

August 24, 2009: Dad Finally Made it to Edwin Shaw! 95

August 24, 2009: Fill My Cup, Lord 96

August 26, 2009: Quick Update 97

August 28, 2009: Edwin Shaw 98

August 30, 2009: Weekend with Dad 100

August 30, 2009: Overcome Evil with Good 103

September 3, 2009: Update on "Walking and Talking" 104

September 4, 2009: Re-Learning Everyday Tasks 105

September 6, 2009: Dad Called Me Today 109

September 07, 2009: A Different Type of Grief 109

September 10, 2009: In An Instant by Bob and Lee Woodruff 116

September 10, 2009: Swallowing Test Results 119

September 11, 2009: Eating for the First Time! 119

September 18, 2009: Preparing to Go Home 122

September 18, 2009: Miracle of the Moment 122

September 21, 2009: Changing of the Seasons 127

September 26, 2009: Visiting Dad at Home 131

October 8, 2009: Dad's New Smile 134

October 11, 2009: Dad's Visit to Findlay 135

October 18, 2009: A Week of Healing 136

October 21, 2009: Saying Goodbye to a Family Friend 141

October 21, 2009: Dad Will Be Visiting Findlay Again 142

October 23, 2009: The Way of Forgiveness 144

October 25, 2009: Ohio State Football 149

October 27, 2009: YMCA Works and the Posture Nazi 150

October 27, 2009: Visits from Friends and Playing the Wii ... 153

October 27, 2009: God is Providing 154

October 28, 2009: Yahtzee and Another Good Day 155

October 30, 2009: Finding My Pony 156

December 6, 2009: Dad's Speech He Wrote and Delivered .. 159

January 30, 2011: An Update 162

The Story Continues... 165

References

[1] Young, Wm. Paul. *The Shack. Where Tragedy Confronts Eternity*. Windblown Media, 2007, 141-142.
[2] *Understanding Brain Injury, A Guide for the Family*. 1999, 2000 Mayo Press
[3] Oakley, Paul. *Father Me*. 2006 Kingsway Music. Manufactured by EMI Christian Music Group.
[4] Barnes, Emilie. *Fill My Cup Lord*. Harvest House Publishers, 2001.
[5] Woodruff, Lee. Woodruff, Bob. *In an Instant: A Family's Journey of Love and Healing*. Random House, 2007, 50.
[6] Ibid, 92.
[7] Ibid, 50.
[8] Young, Sarah. *Jesus Calling: Enjoying Peace in His Presence*. Thomas Nelson. 2004.
[9] Chapman, Steven Curtis. *Miracle of the Moment*. Sparrow Records. 2009. Manufactured by EMI Christian Music Group
[10] Strait, George. *I Saw God Today*. MCA Nashville, a Division of UMG Recordings, Inc. 2008.

www.ingramcontent.com/pod-product-compliance
Lightning Source LLC
Chambersburg PA
CBHW060320050426
42449CB00011B/2572